Pay for Results

*Aligning Executive Compensation
with Business Performance*

Pay for Results

Aligning Executive Compensation with Business Performance

Mercer

WILEY

John Wiley & Sons, Inc.

For general information on our other products and services, or technical support, please contact our Customer Care Department within the United States at 800-762-2974, outside the United States at 317-572-3993 or fax 317-572-4002.

Wiley also publishes its books in a variety of electronic formats. Some content that appears in print may not be available in electronic books.

For more information about Wiley products, visit our Web site at http://www.wiley.com.

Library of Congress Cataloging-in-Publication Data:

Pay for results : aligning executive compensation with business performance / Mercer.
    p. cm.
Includes index.
ISBN 978-0-470-18390-8 (cloth)
    1. Executives—Salaries, etc. 2. Chief executive officers—Salaries, etc. I. Mercer (Firm)
HD4965.2.P39 2009
658.4'072—dc22

2008052081

Printed in the United States of America

10 9 8 7 6 5 4 3 2 1

Contents

Preface

In working with our clients at Mercer, we have emphasized the importance of aligning pay with performance. In fact, we published two prior books on the topic: *Pay for Performance* (2002) and *Responsible Executive Compensation* (2004). So, why another book and why the emphasis on pay for results?

Why Now?

It is no surprise to anyone who reads the newspapers that the corporate governance environment has changed dramatically, even since we published our last book five years ago. Shareholders are demanding that pay be commensurate with outcomes, in a way that is transparent and tangible. In the United States and Canada, the disclosure rules for publicly traded companies require that performance measures be disclosed in most cases and that companies explain how their pay programs relate to organizational performance.

While we have been preparing for publication, the market has continued to focus on this issue, prompted in part by the global economic slowdown. Aligning pay with performance is no longer just important, it is now essential to a responsible executive remuneration program, and that holds true in every major region around the globe.

Woe be the company that ignores the importance of demonstrating to its stakeholders that its CEO's remuneration is linked to company performance. Companies where pay appears disconnected from results are roundly denounced, and their directors find themselves subject to withhold or no vote campaigns in, for example, the United States, or to removal in the United Kingdom and other countries that give shareholders such a right. Regardless of where you are, decision makers, whether board members or CEOs, may find themselves ousted over failing to align pay with results.

Why "Results"?

As a consulting point of view, Mercer is focused on results, rather than performance. This isn't just a semantics change. We want to emphasize that while you can get a pat on the back for effort (which many equate with performance), you should get paid for delivering results—results that over the long term deliver increased value to shareholders and are evaluated in the context of the market and the company's business strategy.

Paying for results necessarily means that a one size remuneration strategy will not fit all. Designing short- or long-term incentive plans to align with results has to be customized to the specific organization, whether corporate entity, business unit, or a division. Too often we see companies migrating to "plain vanilla" measures such as total shareholder return or earnings per share. These are end measures, they do not reflect the drivers of long-term value nor do they communicate to participants the company's strategic or tactical priorities.

Why This Book?

As we observe the market and the seemingly endless string of spectacular failures in the executive pay arena—option backdating, outsized severance packages, huge sign-on or make whole payments for new hires, generous perks and benefits, and the packages associated with the global credit crisis—we believed that boards or executives were not adequately linking reward outcomes to sustainable performance results.

This book gives us the opportunity to reach a broader audience, rather than one client at a time, to provide guidance based on our experience and consulting tools on how to get the pay for results equation right. Our perspective starts with business strategy and takes into account everything from measure selection and target setting to assessing the probabilities of outcomes and how remuneration should be calibrated to ensure that the pay is commensurate with results.

Whether you are in finance, human resources, leading a business unit or corporation, or serving on the board of directors, we believe you will find this book a useful tool to prepare for designing new programs or refining existing ones.

Acknowledgments

Mercer wishes to thank Jennifer Wagner and Jim Sillery for their special contributions to *Pay for Results*. Jim Sillery, a principal formerly with Mercer, works with companies in the areas of global remuneration, executive remuneration, performance measurement and talent management. Jennifer Wagner, an executive remuneration consultant and principal in Mercer's San Francisco office, provided tremendous assistance in helping to write and publish this book (see her biography, on page 224).

Chapter 1

A New Day

*The Call for a Demonstrable Link between Pay
and Performance*

Executive Remuneration Governance

The corporate governance paradigm has shifted dramatically when it comes to a company's executive remuneration. In the past, investors had little voice in what or how executives were paid. In reality, if shareholders were unhappy with executive pay, they had little recourse other than to sell their shares in the company.

Boards of directors did not have much influence either. The stability of boards (the average length of service for directors was well over a decade) often led to a strong sense of trust and comfort with the company's management team and the compensation programs used to reward their contributions. Pay recommendations put forth annually by management would be reviewed for reasonableness and approved by the compensation committee of the board with little independent review of such matters as the peer companies used to evaluate the competitiveness of pay or the inputs used to calibrate performance targets, to the extent targets were even used.

Management tended to take the lead in recommending pay increases, negotiating new employee contracts, and designing new incentive programs. Human resources would collect and analyze benchmark data from published surveys or the proxy statements of peers to assess the competitiveness of the current pay program and develop recommendations for the upcoming year. Finance would be responsible for identifying the performance measures that would fund incentive programs and for calibrating awards with various performance levels based on the internal budget. The bulk of the work was performed in advance of the compensation committee meeting with little direct involvement from directors—the board's blessing often viewed as a necessary informality.

The picture today is strikingly different. Investors around the globe wield significant influence and clamor for more say over executive pay matters. Boards face increased scrutiny from shareholders, the media, and legislators and regulators as they struggle to balance the interests of investors and management. Management is being asked to take a back seat in a process they previously led, and are gradually redefining their role as one of collaboration and consultation.

Investor Role

Governance developments vary by region, but we are experiencing a definite increase in shareholder influence on executive remuneration issues from Europe to North America to Asia Pacific and beyond. There is little doubt this trend will continue as shareholders react to the widespread share price declines that have resulted from the economic downturn.

Shareholders in Europe have been leading the charge. Beginning in 2003, public companies in the United Kingdom were required to give shareholders an advisory up-or-down vote on executive remuneration packages. While this "say-on-pay" vote is nonbinding in the United Kingdom, proponents argue that it has increased the dialogue between companies and large investors and has brought about changes in compensation practices that have improved the alignment between pay and performance. For example, share option plans—criticized for rewarding short-term share price volatility over long-term value creation—have been largely replaced with performance-contingent stock grants among U.K. companies.

Several countries in continental Europe have also adopted legislation that gives shareholders a voice on executive remuneration matters— and, in some cases, the votes are binding. Investors in the Netherlands, Sweden, and Norway cast a binding vote on executive pay and some firms in Spain and Switzerland have voluntarily introduced advisory votes. Across Europe, companies are making efforts to improve the disclosure of their executive remuneration programs.

European governments are trying to exert more direct influence over executive pay arrangements as well. A new measure in France requires that severance payments be conditional on performance—a practice essentially unheard of until now. Meanwhile, legislators in the Netherlands want to limit nonperformance-based compensation by imposing an additional tax on salary and severance payments that exceed €500,000. In the wake of the financial crisis and global economic downturn, these types of caps may well become more commonplace.

Following the U.K. lead, Australia instituted a nonbinding, advisory vote on executive remuneration for public companies beginning in 2005. While the large majority of companies receive a positive vote, there have been a few notable exceptions. Where "no" votes occurred, the protests sent a clear message to the board and management, prompting some companies to change their remuneration programs. Others looked to pacify shareholders by improving transparency around the compensation decision-making process and providing more meaningful exchanges with major investors.

North American countries have been notably behind the curve on governance reforms, but there has been more activity in this area in recent years. Both the United States and Canada have adopted new disclosure rules that provide additional information to shareholders on executive remuneration programs and practices and improve comparability across companies. Initial compliance with the new rules was spotty, but the situation appears to be improving as the regulatory bodies in each country work to clarify their expectations.

Institutional shareholders in the United States and Canada have also been submitting an increasing number of proposals on compensation matters as part of the annual shareholder vote. While most of these proposals have so far failed to get a majority vote, say-on-pay resolutions have been garnering increased support and passed at a handful of U.S. companies in 2008. These proposals are likely to be prevalent again in the 2009 proxy season and may receive much stronger support sparked by the economic downturn. Fueling the development is the rise in influence of proxy advisory groups, which are (not surprisingly) advocating of more direct shareholder involvement in executive remuneration matters.

U.S. legislators have also been looking for ways to curb executive compensation abuses, including proposing say-on-pay requirements and limiting the use of certain types of compensation. They passed legislation that restricts the use of nonqualified deferred compensation, and the deteriorating economic situation (including the international bailout of the financial sector and associated restrictions on executive compensation payouts) is bringing further impetus to the call for widespread reform.

While companies in emerging markets have largely escaped these pressures, many are taking a proactive stance and developing responsible disclosure practices in line with those in more mature markets. Companies in China, India, and other growing economies are also looking for ways to strengthen the link between pay and performance by introducing performance-based incentives.

Board Role

Stemming from a more activist shareholder base and heightened media attention, the board role is in the midst of transition. We are seeing a shift in the board's accountability from high-level oversight of the business—including executive remuneration matters—to independent review and verification of corporate strategy and more direct involvement in day-to-day decision making.

This increase in responsibility means a greater time commitment for compensation committee members. Committees are upping the number of times they meet each year and asking directors to spend larger amounts of time preparing for meetings, reviewing materials, or participating in preliminary discussions. Because the regulatory environment has become more complex over the years, directors have had to invest additional time in training on executive remuneration matters—both up-front (upon appointment to the committee) and ongoing, in order to keep up with the constantly changing rules and regulations. The role of the committee chair has also expanded to fill the need for greater collaboration with outside advisors, as well as with management.

Greater scrutiny of the board role (along with a few visible shareholder lawsuits following major corporate scandals) has increased the perceived liability associated with the director position. This has pushed many boards to adopt a risk-management mentality in managing their fiduciary responsibilities. Directors must constantly weigh how their decisions impact the business *and* how they appear to shareholders. It is no longer simply a matter of showing that compensation levels are reasonable; boards today must be able to rationalize why the compensation package looks the way it does. They must defend why one equity vehicle was selected over another, explain how performance metrics support shareholder value creation, point out the specific inputs that went into the annual target setting process, and prove why selected peers are valid comparators for compensation benchmarking.

Boards have to balance the pressure on pay from shareholders with the need to attract and retain top executive talent. This has become harder than ever. Merger and acquisition activity has resulted in larger and larger organizations, and few individuals have the skills and experience to run businesses of this size and scope. The move toward privatization has also compounded the talent shortage, with many top executives lured away from the public sector market by highly leveraged pay packages offered by private equity investors.

Globalization is also having a profound affect on the ability of companies to attract and retain executive talent. Executives are increasingly willing to move across borders to greener pastures, so companies must often compete not only within their home country, but also against foreign competitors for talent. Meanwhile, firms expanding into new markets sometimes find it difficult to recruit executives in the local market because what is status quo to shareholders in the home country might not be competitive or attractive in other regions. For example, companies in the United Kingdom that exclusively use performance-based equity can find it difficult to recruit talent from the United States, where equity has traditionally vested based on service.

While some boards have welcomed the growing power of shareholders over compensation matters as a counterpoint to management influence, there is no doubt that it has made the process more complex and sensitive. Given the range of interests that must be attended to, many boards are struggling to balance what shareholders want to see with the practical needs of the business.

Management Role

Mirroring the growing influence of shareholders, management control over executive remuneration programs has declined. This is not to say that senior leaders no longer have input into compensation decisions, but long gone are the days where executives called the shots. As boards respond to shareholder concerns by becoming more actively involved in both executive remuneration strategy and implementation, philosophical questions abound as to whether executive remuneration falls under the realm of management or is primarily a governance concern.

Where the pendulum will settle is difficult to predict, but what is clear is that executives feel the heat. Many chief executive officers (CEOs) find themselves playing "defense" when it comes to executive remuneration matters and are being forced to invest greater amounts of time and resources into building the business case behind pay decisions. This development can be troubling to senior leadership because it is their responsibility to achieve positive business results, and they know more than anyone that the right executive talent can make or break a company's best efforts.

While executive talent can be one of the most important investments a company can make, the line between competitive and excessive remuneration can be a difficult one to walk—especially if remuneration decisions can be criticized as self-serving. In this regard, the additional pressure on management to demonstrate that compensation programs are reasonable and defensible should bring more accountability to the process.

However, executives must retain the flexibility to make timely decisions that are responsive to both internal and external developments impacting the company's talent strategy. Executives need the ability to respond quickly and decisively to retention concerns. Directors, who are not involved in day-to-day business operations, are usually not in the best position to spot emerging retention issues, and obviously this is information that shareholders would not be privy to until it was too late.

Another potential danger is the tendency to fall back on the status quo when designing incentive plans. Shareholders like simple, conventional approaches to incentive compensation because it allows them to more easily compare outcomes across companies. Widely accepted program designs often seem like a safer bet to directors as well, since they pose fewer challenges when it comes to shareholder communication than a customized plan that has been designed to reflect a company's unique business context. In fact, we have already seen this move to standardize programs take place in the United Kingdom and Australia, where institutional investors have pushed companies to link the vesting of long-term equity awards to performance as measured by just a few generic metrics—namely earnings per share or relative total shareholder return measured against peers.

As you will learn from this book, incentive compensation can be an invaluable tool for aligning executive efforts with the strategic priorities of the business. While an easily understood plan that allows for more direct comparisons against peers might be welcomed by shareholders, it can problematic for the CEO who wants to rally his or her team behind a new revenue or return goal in support of the company's business strategy. Just as a manufacturing company that seeks to lower costs by commoditizing its products must consider the impact on customer demand, gains from streamlining the measurement and reward processes across companies must be balanced against the ability of companies to tailor measurement and reward processes to their specific needs.

Achieving the Right Balance of Interests

While the balance of power in the realm of executive remuneration matters used to lie squarely in the hands of the executive team, it has undergone a historic shift away from management and toward shareholders. The full consequences of this transition have yet to be revealed. Some correction of the power imbalance was clearly necessary and should lead to positive reforms, but, as with all transformations—organizational, political, social, or economic—we must be wary of unintended consequences.

Let us start with the positive. Across mature markets, we already see more dialogue with key investors (particularly the institutional shareholder base) as companies seek to incorporate their views and objectives into their governance and compensation policies and practices. We can also expect more collaborative executive remuneration programs, which reflect innovative practices drawing on investor input and experience and a greater focus on calibrated pay-for-performance plans and arrangements. Other likely developments include more transparent disclosure, the curbing of excessive nonperformance-based executive benefits programs and large severance guarantees, and more meaningful performance conditions being attached to incentive compensation.

On the flip side, greater involvement on the part of shareholders could become a bureaucratic nightmare if not kept in check. Lengthy proxy battles over director nominees or executive remuneration matters can be prohibitively expensive, especially for smaller companies, and may actually be counterproductive to the objective of shareholder value creation. Greater dissent in the boardroom will also increase the cost of governance and may hamper a company's ability to respond to developments quickly and nimbly. Under the worst-case scenario, governance headaches may usher in a new age of privatization, as companies look for ways to free up resources and streamline decision-making processes, as we have already seen to some extent with Sarbanes-Oxley in the United States.

To maintain the right balance in control over executive remuneration matters, shareholders, directors, and management must have clearly delineated objectives, roles, and responsibilities. Shareholders must find the right balance between holding the board accountable and trying to seize control. They need to be vocal in demanding alignment between shareholder value and executive pay, but should avoid unnecessarily hamstringing the organization. For example, in the United Kingdom and Australia, shareholder activism has severely limited the flexibility companies have to design customized rewards programs and has led to an overreliance on cookie-cutter incentive plans that provide little connection to company-specific business strategy.

Meanwhile, the board must carefully balance shareholder concerns with the strategic and operating needs of the business. Directors must consistently demonstrate proper due diligence and exercise thoughtful and defensible decision-making. They must make a real commitment to clear and transparent disclosure and promote open lines of communication with both executives and shareholders.

Boards also need to find the right balance between oversight and micromanagement when dealing with the executive team. They should independently verify incentive plan payouts, ask tough questions about plan design, and provide objective input and guidance on compensation matters based on their knowledge and experience. Yet, the board may not always be in the best position to spearhead design work or facilitate plan administration, and must be willing to turn over the reins to the executive team when it makes the most sense to do so.

For their part, management must find the right balance between ownership and collaboration. Executives have on-the-ground knowledge and should be actively involved in driving remuneration decisions, but they must also be open to independent review and critique. They should be prepared to explain and defend their point of view and be flexible enough to shift their approach when necessary. They must also exhibit a strong focus on shareholder interests by aligning executive remuneration programs with value creation and rewarding sustainable, long-term results instead of short-term spikes in performance.

Greater shareholder involvement will no doubt be a powerful force in shaping executive remuneration, but it is not a panacea. Remuneration continues to rise in countries where say-on-pay policies have been adopted because the fact remains that an effective management team is critical to business success and there are far too few talented executives to go around. Executive pay is an art, not a science, and it is impossible to agree upon a perfect definition. The best companies can do is to make reasonable decisions based on thorough analysis and meaningful collaboration among stakeholders. Performance measurement is the key to making this a reality.

Performance Measurement as the Key to Good Governance

There are many factors that influence how smoothly the system of governance functions in an organization. You must have clarity of roles and effective division of labor. There must be an appropriate investment of time and resources and a well-rounded and flexible process for decision making. Directors and executives must exhibit leadership, while at the same time be able to work as team members when collaboration is called for. They must also possess deep knowledge of the business and have a thorough understanding of the factors influencing the market in which they operate.

When it comes to executive remuneration governance, all of these things are important, but a solid performance measurement system is, perhaps, the single strongest determinant of whether or not stakeholder interests will be met. Performance measurement serves as the basis on which decisions are made and judged and provides a common language for communicating the goals of the organization so as to align everyone behind shared objectives. This helps position the company for long-term, sustainable value creation; not surprisingly, high-performing companies tend to have fewer problems in the governance arena.

Performance measurement is important to shareholders, directors, and executives alike. Each of these stakeholders has different priorities when it comes to monitoring and rewarding results, and the most effective measurement systems will be responsive to a wide range of interests (Exhibit 1.1).

The goal of this book is to help compensation committees, senior leaders, and human resources professionals develop a balanced and defensible approach to performance measurement—one that fairly and accurately captures results so that companies can more confidently reward executive contributions.

Change Is in the Air

Besides the shifting governance paradigm, there have been many other developments that have shaped the executive remuneration environment over the past decade. While these vary from region to region, they

What Investors Want	What the Board Wants	What Management Wants
• Clear and transparent disclosure of performance standards and compensation decisions.	• Simplicity and ease of communication.	• Strong line of sight to individual behavior.
• Direct linkage to shareholder value creation.	• Reasonable, defensible pay and performance outcomes.	• Alignment with the business strategy and other organizational processes (no cookie-cutter metrics).
• Meaningful performance contingencies and fair calibration between results and payouts (no free rides).	• Flexibility to address both retention and measurement challenges as they arise.	• Motivational goals that contain the right amount of "stretch."

Exhibit 1.1   Stakeholder Objectives of Performance Measurement
SOURCE: Mercer.

encompass such things as converging accounting practices, enhanced disclosure, and heightened attention on executive perquisites, benefits, and severance arrangements.

The impact of these changes has been widespread. While trends have played out differently in different regions, some common themes have emerged:

- Increased focus on variable remuneration.
- Shift from stock options to full value shares.
- Greater use of performance-based equity.
- Elimination of egregious perquisites and benefits, including tax gross-ups.
- Imposed limits on nonperformance-based pay, including severance and change-in-control benefits, supplemental executive retirement, and deffered compensation.
- Greater diversity in remuneration packages.

These developments are moving executive remuneration practices in the right direction. Around the globe companies are taking a more comprehensive approach to executive remuneration design and making strides to improve the link between pay and performance. From increasing the use of variable pay to attaching performance conditions to long-term incentives, executive remuneration programs are becoming more balanced and more responsible.

Pay for Performance Today

To get a better sense for how these trends are playing out in the marketplace, let us review current practices in mature and developing markets. (For a more targeted look at executive remuneration hot topics internationally, see Exhibit 1.2 "Snapshot of Executive Remuneration around the Globe.")

Pay Mix

In mature markets, executive remuneration is delivered primarily through variable pay. This means a significant portion of the remuneration opportunity is at risk and is contingent upon achieving positive performance results. Both short-term incentives (typically an annual cash bonus plan) and long-term incentives (generally some form of equity) are prevalent in the market place, with a greater emphasis on long-term remuneration at most organizations (particularly in the United States where companies continue to rely heavily on equity-based remuneration).

Companies in developing countries, such as those in Latin America and Asia, tend to rely more heavily on fixed remuneration, such as base salary and executive benefits, although the use of both cash and equity incentives is growing.

Short-Term Incentive Remuneration

Short-term incentives are highly leveraged in mature markets. In the United States, annual executive bonus opportunities typically range from 50 to 200 percent of salary, sometimes reaching upward of 300 percent of base salary at maximum. In the United Kingdom and other mature markets, maximum annual bonus levels have traditionally been lower but are now trending upward.

Short-term bonuses are also relatively common in emerging markets. However, such opportunities typically represent a smaller portion of the total pay package. Economic uncertainty in these regions can make it difficult to set goals even one year out, so shorter performance periods (quarterly, semiannual) are sometimes used.

	Canada	Australia	Latin America
What characterizes executive remuneration in the region today?	• Use of multiple long-term incentive vehicles to achieve complementary objectives, each with differing time periods, performance measures and emphasis on performance vs. retention. • Increased rigor in the selection of performance measures, and the calibration and "stress-testing" of targets.	• A high proportion of incentives linked to performance goals and a balanced approach to incentives that avoids excessive risk taking. • Nonbinding vote on executive pay has increased transparency and allows shareholders to express their views, while leaving final decision making in the hands of the board. • Dual performance hurdles for long-term incentives are becoming more common (e.g., relative TSR coupled with strategic goals in areas like customer service and risk management).	• Weak link between compensation and performance due to heavy reliance on base pay. • Scarce use of equity or other long-term incentives focuses management resources on short-term, rather than long-term results. • Budding interest in the use of performance share plans.
What are the key challenges facing companies as they seek to improve the link between pay and performance?	• Finding sufficient, suitable Canadian comparators for pay and performance benchmarking can be difficult and is leading to the consideration of non-Canadian comparators where the Canadian market is too thin. • Balancing paying for performance with need to attract and retain top-flight talent continues to be a challenge in light of increased scrutiny. • The "boom or bust" nature of commodity-based industries makes it difficult for some Canadian companies to set meaningful performance goals.	• Growing shareholder influence stemming from say-on-pay requirement indirectly limits flexibility in plan design and has prompted many companies to adopt a wait-and-see approach when it comes to performance measurement. • Uncertain economic outlook has resulted in increased pressure from executives for boards to revisit STI and LTI hurdles. Boards need to exercise caution and carefully consider how economic conditions versus management performance impact performance prospects.	• A turbulent economic environment—high inflation, economic uncertainty, etc.—makes it difficult to plan beyond the short term, which tends to limit plan design. • Stock price appreciation is an unreliable executive performance measure because Latin American stocks are heavily influenced by exogenous factors. Careful assessment of market risk is needed to calibrate the delicate balance between risk and reward in equity-based incentive plans.
What developments should companies watch for going forward?	• New executive compensation disclosure rules will continue to put the spotlight on pay and performance alignment, equity and pension values, and termination and change-of-control benefits. • Modest but continued say-on-pay activism may impact board decision-making processes and compensation program design. • Impact of economic and governance developments in the U.S. likely to flow over into Canada.	• Further disclosure and regulation of executive pay are being discussed but would result in additional complexities and constraints on boards' ability to set remuneration policy in line with company structure and business strategy. • Greater focus on succession planning and leadership development is likely, as it is becoming imperative to develop executive talent from within.	• Upward pressure on executive pay, the desire to contain fixed compensation, and demands for improved performance are causing the variable or "at risk" component of executive pay packages to increase as a proportion of total compensation. • Gravitation toward U.S.-style approach (particularly the greater use of equity) is expected, despite cultural and economic differences. • Companies are expected to pay more attention to reward delivery and the connection between senior management's short- and long-term impact on business performance and shareholder value.

Exhibit 1.2 Snapshot of Executive Remuneration around the Globe

SOURCE: Mercer.

There is significant variety in short-term performance measurement practices from company to company, but some common themes emerge:

- Profitability metrics are the most common measures of short-term performance around the globe.
- Most companies use more than one metric to measure performance in their annual incentive plans.
- Strategic objectives are often used in combination with financial metrics.
- Measuring results against absolute goals is more common than relative performance measurement.

Long-Term Incentive Remuneration

The use of multiple equity vehicles to deliver long-term incentive remuneration has become commonplace in mature markets, although the long-term incentive mix varies by region. For example, time-vested stock options continue to be prevalent in the United States (Exhibit 1.3.) and Canada, but have declined in use in the United Kingdom and Australia. A portfolio-style approach is beneficial to both executives and shareholders because it adds balance to the overall remuneration program design and increases the likelihood that remuneration outcomes will be fair and reasonable in light of performance.

Long-term performance measurement practices also tend to fall along regional lines. Companies in North America have significant flexibility in designing long-term incentive programs, and metrics include everything from revenue to economic profit to share price goals (Exhibit 1.4). In the United Kingdom and Australia, there is more consistency in practice as a result of institutional shareholder guidance. Companies in these regions tend to vest performance shares or options based on the achievement of earnings per share goals or relative total shareholder return measured against industry peers (Exhibit 1.5).

The use of long-term incentives has been much less prevalent in emerging markets. In some regions, such as China, regulatory restrictions make it difficult to implement equity programs. In other regions, market volatility has hindered the motivational value of equity, while unstable economic conditions have historically made

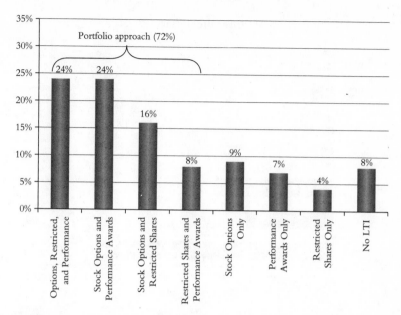

Exhibit 1.3 CEO Equity Delivery among 350 Large and Midsize U.S. Companies

SOURCE: Mercer.

NOTE: Market data reflects information pulled from the most recent proxy statements of 350 large and midsize public companies in the United States across a range of industries.

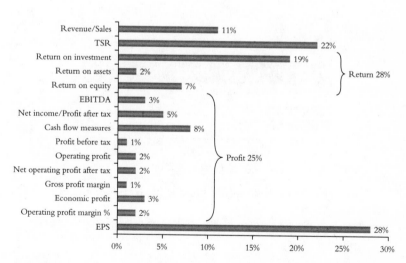

Exhibit 1.4 Metrics Used in Performance-Based Long-Term Incentive Plans (U.S.)

SOURCE: Mercer.

NOTE: Market data reflects information pulled from the most recent proxy statements of 350 large and midsize public companies in the United States across a range of industries.

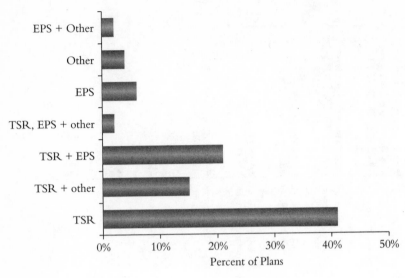

Performance Share Plans

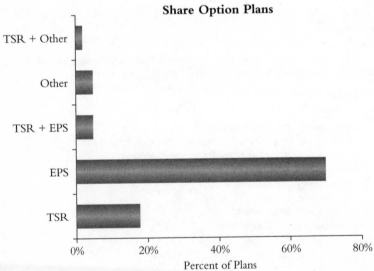

Share Option Plans

Exhibit 1.5   Metrics Used in Performance-Based Long-Term Incentive Plans (U.K.)

SOURCE: Mercer

NOTE: Market data reflects information pulled from the public filings of the FTSE 100 companies.

long-term goal setting a challenge. The tides are turning, however, and a growing number of companies in these regions are looking to add a long-term component to the total executive remuneration package.

The Verdict

How successful have the design changes outlined here been in improving the link between pay and results? Research on the relationship between pay and performance among large and midsize companies in the United States suggests that there continues to be room for improvement. Overall, year-over-year changes in total direct remuneration (base salary plus actual bonus payouts plus expected long-term incentive values) appear to be reasonably well aligned with performance (Exhibit 1.6). However, remuneration levels were up for more than half of the "bottom" performers, suggesting that companies could better balance upside opportunity with more meaningful downside risk.

The bottom line is that companies are on the right track, but in order for programmatic changes—like adopting performance-based equity—to really enhance the pay for performance relationship, companies need to get performance measurement right.

Bringing Defensibility to Executive Remuneration

Without a sound performance measurement system, it is impossible to assess the reasonableness of executive remuneration programs and payouts. You must know whether or not the company is creating shareholder value and the degree to which that value creation (or destruction) can be attributed to executive performance.

This book is intended to bring your measurement practices and, by extension, your executive remuneration programs to a new level. It aims to give boards, management teams, and human resources professions the tools they need to:

- Abandon the guesswork and start making informed decisions based on hard research, in-depth quantitative analysis, and intelligent discussion.

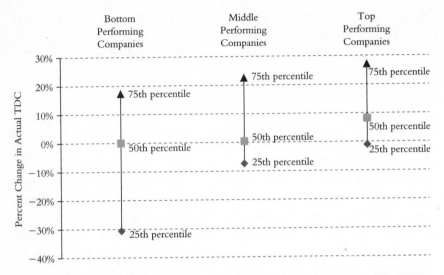

Exhibit 1.6. Actual Total Direct Remuneration by Performance Group (U.S.)
Source: Mercer.
Note: Market data reflects information pulled from the most recent proxy statements of 350 large and midsize public companies in the United States across a range of industries. Companies were divided into three performance groups based on comparative financial results as measured by five key metrics (revenue growth, net income growth, EBITDA margin, ROI, and TSR).

- Stop working backward by agreeing on a definition of value for your organization up front—and then identifying those factors that have the greatest impact on its creation.
- Use the business strategy as the basis for selecting performance metrics, rather than relying heavily on what competitors or analysts tell you to measure.
- Use both internal planning and external trends and economic data to set performance targets that will motivate your executive team to shine—and let your shareholders sleep at night.
- Test the relationship between award and performance levels thoroughly to make sure that pay outcomes will be reasonable under all performance scenarios—both strong and weak.
- Make your measurement system a high-impact one by anticipating problems before they happen and investing the necessary time and resources in implementation.

Change is in the air, and companies must meet the challenge of performance measurement head on to ensure that their remuneration programs are reasonable and defensible to all stakeholders. When times are good, it is less critical to have a perfect measurement system, but during more difficult times, the stakes are bigger and companies simply cannot afford to be wrong. Directors and management need to partner together to make pay for performance a reality before shareholders take matters into their own hands.

Chapter 2

The Million Dollar Question

What Is Good Performance?

Nearly every company espouses a "pay for performance" philosophy, but how exactly does one go about defining performance? It is easy enough to say you know good performance when you see it, but subjective judgments after the fact are not enough. Shareholders and executives alike want to know what criteria are being used to evaluate performance and, in order for incentives to effectively motivate behavior, those criteria must be defined in advance.

At the most basic level, performance consists of two elements: the efforts and behaviors that an executive puts in and observable results that are the outcomes of those efforts. Best efforts are well and good, but at the executive level, shareholders demand results. The ultimate result that every public company strives for is the creation of shareholder value. As such, among public companies, positive *total shareholder return* (TSR) is often relied upon as evidence of good performance. If your stock price is going up and your company is paying out dividends, the reasoning goes that your executives must be doing something right.

Unfortunately, the relationship between total shareholder return and executive performance is not that clear. Every investor knows that stock price is the product of innumerable factors, some specific to the company and others more exogenous in nature. Companies can benefit from a rise in the market as a whole, such as occurs following a drop in interest rates. Of course, the reverse can happen too—a lesson many companies learned as they watched stock prices tumble in response to the financial industry meltdown. Stock prices can also be impacted by conditions in the industry that may or may not reflect the company's actual results or prospects.

Even if the rise in stock price can be attributed to firm-specific factors, it can be difficult to ascertain the extent to which executive behaviors actually caused the increase. What portion of the success can be attributed to executive leadership versus management execution? What were the roles of specific business units or functional groups in bringing about the change? Was the increase in share price the result of a team effort? Or can we give credit to specific individuals?

At the same time, a drop in shareholder value is not always indicative of poor performance. During an economic downturn or an industry down cycle, shareholder value may be declining across the board. Yet, some companies will do a better job weathering the storm and preserving shareholder value than others. In cases like this, good performance must be defined differently.

There is also the matter of timing. Business results that are strategic in nature are often not immediately reflected in external valuations. Consider a renewal company that is reinvesting to rebuild its franchise. Profits and returns may be hurt in the short-term, and investors may respond prematurely by selling off shares. The dip in stock price, however, reflects activities that are actually positive and essential to ensure the long-term success of the business.

Clearly, "good" performance is not always as great as it seems, and "poor" performance is sometimes not so terrible. Results that intuitively seem positive or negative can often be misleading and, depending on how you analyze it, financial or market data can be manipulated to support predetermined conclusions or paint a rosier picture than actually exists. The challenge lies not in defining "good" performance, but rather in defining "real" performance—that is, pinpointing the results that capture real value creation.

Defining real performance requires balancing the competing interests of different stakeholders and taking into consideration a wide variety of measurement perspectives. It calls for objective data, gathered through in-depth research and analysis, and an effective decision-making process for synthesizing the information and drawing accurate conclusions about the real value created. Most importantly, however, it demands a thorough understanding of your business, because in the end, performance cannot be defined unless it is within the context of the results that are intended to be brought about. In this chapter, we discuss these requirements for capturing value creation and bring to light other factors that companies should consider in order to define performance measurement in terms that make sense for their own unique organization.

Performance as Value Creation

There are an infinite number of ways to measure performance. Performance can be measured based on stock price or earnings per share. It can be assessed against internal budgets or relative to peers. It can be measured over a single financial quarter, a year, a decade, or even the entire life of the business. Regardless of the methods used, the objective is the same: to capture the amount of value that has been created.

Value creation applies to all types of organizations, from public companies to not-for-profit organizations and government agencies. The purpose of every organization is to generate some sort of value for its constituents, and your assessment of performance must be grounded in an understanding of the types of value you intend to create.

Organizations generate multiple types of value, so it is helpful to begin by identifying the individuals or groups that stand to benefit from such value creation. We call these constituents *stakeholders* since they share risks and opportunities through their association with the organization, although these risks and opportunities (and the relationship between the two) may vary considerably.

In the case of a for-profit company, stakeholders can be separated into several broad categories, including shareholders, employees, customers, business partners, the community, and governing bodies (Exhibit 2.1). These categories can be further refined, since, for example, employees at various levels of the organization have very different risks and opportunities associated with their employment. In addition, the interests of some constituents will span more than one category. In fact, this is the crux of executive ownership initiatives that seek to put equity in the hands of senior management so that their interests will be more closely aligned with the interests of shareholders.

Shareholders include founders of the business, early providers of capital, employees awarded shares of the company as remuneration, investors who have purchased shares on the public market, and financial entities (such as mutual funds, hedge funds or pension managers) that have assets invested in the company. For shareholders, value creation results from an increase in the enterprise value of the firm. At publicly traded companies, enterprise value (as measured externally) is generated

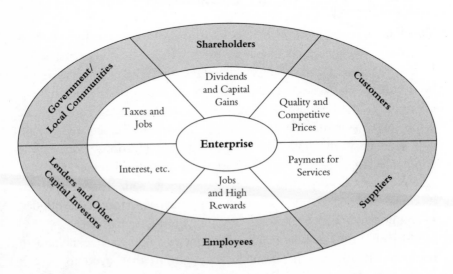

Exhibit 2.1 Stakeholders in a For-Profit Company
Source: Mercer.

by increases in stock price or the payment of dividends. At private companies, enterprise value is tied to dividends paid or increases in asset value.

Value can be defined differently for shareholders, depending on their focus and the nature of their investment. A sustained incremental increase in enterprise value as measured by total shareholder return is typically seen as the end goal for shareholders in a publicly traded company. Yet, more speculative investors with shorter time horizons will look to other indicators of performance, like volatility, to guide their investment decisions. Financial investors in privately held companies, like private equity firms or venture capitalists, use metrics like free cash flow to assess the economic value of the company. Meanwhile, strategic investors that are adding platform companies to their portfolio will look for evidence that the company is leveraging their core assets—or missing critical opportunities.

For employees of the company, value is usually defined through employment considerations and remuneration arrangements. Executives want a competitive remuneration package that provides an appropriate balance between upside opportunity and downside risk. They also want there to be strong line of sight between their actions and the rewards they receive, and they want incentives to be aligned with controllable business drivers, rather than factors outside of their control.

Below the management level, employees seek a comfortable balance between opportunity and security. They want to be sure their basic financial and welfare needs are met, but they also value shared destinies and rewards that are linked to the fortunes of the larger organization. In addition, employees want to work in a culture that recognizes and respects their contributions and they want advancement opportunities that will enable them to develop their skills and grow professionally over the course of their career.

Value for customers is determined by how well the products or services provided by the company meet their needs. Customers want business strategies that recognize their voice on matters such as design, pricing, customization, and delivery and companies will want to consider how customer experience should factor into business planning and performance measurement.

Business partners derive value from a relationship that is transparent and fair. They want business strategies that send consistent signals and, while they want the partner company to be successful, they do not want profits to be created by shifting risks and costs to them. Providers of capital, such as banks, similarly want to work with financially sound companies so that they may receive a reasonable rate of interest on their loans, paid in a timely manner.

The local community values the prestige and potential charity and public service that come from having a successful company in the area. The government values the generation of tax revenue, as well as the economic benefits that result from the creation of stable, high-paying jobs.

The reality is that value is defined in many different ways and stakeholders are inevitably interested in maximizing their own value. Yet, it is impossible to create shareholder value without the active cooperation of employees, customers, business partners, community groups, and government entities. On the flipside, research indicates that companies that perform well for shareholders tend to deliver greater value to other stakeholders, while companies that fail to generate sufficient value for shareholders are often unable to competitively reward employees, respond to customer needs through product and service innovation, maintain stable business relationships, or create jobs and tax revenue over the long-term. This suggests an intersection of interests around the objective of shareholder value creation.

By aligning diverse perspectives to a common outcome, shareholders' perceptions on value can serve as a proxy for all other stakeholders. Put another way, maximizing shareholder value can become an effective singular objective for the business, while value generation for other stakeholder groups can be seen as a means for effectively reaching that end.

Focusing on shareholder value as the ultimate business objective has benefits from an organizational process standpoint as well. It enables people to work together toward a common goal, rather than working in a fragmented or contradictory manner and provides a basis for making difficult decisions, such as evaluating trade-offs in resource allocation. It can also empower employees to identify and pursue new opportunities by providing a universal definition of success.

Interestingly, the importance of these concepts is further reinforced when applied to not-for-profit organizations, such as public sector entities, educational institutions, health care organizations, and charitable groups. For these companies, shareholder value creation also serves as the ultimate goal, although shareholders must be thought about much differently. In for-profit companies, shareholders are essentially the "owners" of the business, but who are the "owners" of a university or a hospital? The community is generally the best approximation of shareholders and the value created for the community, whether defined narrowly or in broad terms, will become the overriding goal of the organization.

No Magic Number

Once you have determined the value that your organization intends to create, you must identify ways to measure this value. This requires sifting through numerous facts and figures in order to hone in on those results that are most closely aligned with value creation. There is no magic number that you can rely upon to provide the insight necessary to assess company and executive performance, although some are better than others. Ideally, you must pick and choose from a variety of measurement approaches, each with its own benefits and limitations.

We have already discussed the problems that can arise from relying on absolute TSR as the sole measure of performance. What about accounting measures? Companies must conform to *generally accepted accounting principles* (GAAP) in reporting financial assets and business transactions. In fact, an entire industry exists around confirming the accuracy of accounting statements. Given the rigor and scrutiny involved, it would seem that accounting metrics might serve as an objective basis for measuring performance.

While they do provide valuable information about the financial health of a company, accounting figures alone cannot really tell you whether or not value is being created for your stakeholders. Because accounting principles force companies to conform to a standard set of rules on matters such as depreciation, adjustments are often needed to capture true financial results given the business context. Accounting statements also do a relatively poor job of lining up investments and returns; companies can invest money to generate higher revenues and profits, but in the end, if the projects do not provide a rate of return that exceeds the cost of capital then value has actually been destroyed, rather than created.

In addition, the assessment of accounting metrics requires a frame of reference for judging the results. Whether internal (e.g., internal budget) or external (e.g., peer comparisons) in nature, such comparative analyses involve some degree of subjectivity. For example, many companies compare performance against the annual budget to determine if the company is meeting or falling short of its business objectives. Yet, measuring performance against budget is not a truly objective process; exceeding budget by 10 percent at one company may represent far better performance than the same results at another. The first company may have established very aggressive goals that required drastic improvements over the prior year, while the latter company may have underestimated the company's potential and set the budget at a level that was relatively easy to achieve. Or, the first company may have had to overcome a major obstacle that hurt prospects for the entire industry, while the latter company was helped by an unexpected windfall that was outside of senior management's control.

Given these limitations, some companies have turned to relative performance measurement as a more impartial way to assess results. If you compare your financial results against peers and you have done better than most, you can be confident that you have performed well. Yet, this process has the potential for bias as well. What measures were used, and how well do these measures align with value creation for your stakeholders? How were peer companies selected? Do you have a sufficient representation of the market, and are peers similar enough to your own company to ensure equitable comparisons?

To transcend the limitations of standard accounting metrics, companies can consider more complex measurement approaches. Economic metrics, such as cash flow value added or economic profit, enhance the accuracy of accounting figures by incorporating additional information and making adjustments to the data to isolate real performance results. These measures do a better job capturing value creation because they reveal the extent to which business returns exceed the cost of investments. And, because the cost of capital can be used as an objective baseline for judging value creation, economic measures do not rely on subjective decisions associated with accounting-based measures (such as establishing budgets or selecting peers).

While economic metrics tend to be more accurate at judging real performance than accounting metrics, they still may not translate into value *realized* by shareholders. This is due to the fact that there are several forces that affect external valuations besides current business performance. All companies are impacted by market and industry risk, which influence the shareholder value part and parcel with firm-specific factors. Expectations regarding future performance and intangibles, such as a company's organizational architecture, human capital, and work processes, also play a significant role in driving shareholder value.

In determining the appropriate performance metric, companies must often balance the need for simplicity against the need for technical accuracy (Exhibit 2.2). Companies must also decide whether the metric is being chosen to drive the creation of value or to measure the value that has been created. We discuss these trade-offs in more detail in the next chapter.

Given the variety of factors that influence shareholder experience, it is important for companies to measure the strategic activities necessary to generate value going forward. This requires an assessment of strategic accomplishments and their alignment with the company's business strategy. Unfortunately, this can be a difficult prospect since many strategic initiatives are qualitative in nature. To make the evaluation process less subjective, strategic goals should be defined in measureable terms and tied to a specific time line. And, since strategic accomplishments may not succeed in generating value even if executed properly, they must be carefully balanced with financial and market measures to ensure accountability in the performance measurement process.

An example of the difficulty in setting strategic goals was demonstrated recently when the CEO of a company held a review of strategic initiatives as part of the year-end bonus determination process. In

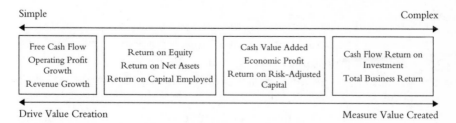

Exhibit 2.2 Trade-Offs of Performance Measure Selection
Source: Mercer.

a self-assessment, the Marketing Director rated his efforts as above aver-age for delivering a new product marketing strategy two weeks early. "I would agree with your assessment," replied the CEO, "if what you presented was what we were looking for." The Marketing Director had assumed that the goal was an event—turning in the marketing strategy. The CEO's view was different. She viewed the goal as receiving a plan that could move the company's business strategy forward.

Sustained value creation is the product of many different factors over time. It cannot be accurately measured by relying on stock price alone—or net income or economic profit or any other single metric, for that matter. Capturing real performance is a complex endeavor that demands a multifaceted measurement approach that is tailored to the organization.

Requirements for Effective Performance Measurement

Imagine you attended a long-distance race and someone asked you if the competitors had run far enough to break the record. You would require several inputs to answer satisfactorily. You would need to select a metric to describe the distance that had been run (for example, kil-ometers) and develop a process for tracking the metric. You would want to ask which competitors were in question—the lead runner, the lead-ing half of competitors, or all of the participants. You would also need to know the previous record, so that you could compare it to the cur-rent results. Finally, you would need to know if there was any limitation to the amount of time the competitors were allowed to run.

As with evaluating the results of a distance race, there are certain requirements necessary to measure business and executive performance:

- *Performance metric selection.* The measures used as an indicator of success.
- *Linkage.* The organizational level (e.g., corporate, business unit, functional group, individual) to which the measure applies.
- *Goal-setting.* The desired level of performance on the selected measures.
- *Time horizon.* The period of time over which performance is measured.

Getting each of these elements right will enable your company to accurately assess performance results. A well-designed performance measurement system can also help drive business results. By focusing efforts on key metrics and setting internal performance targets that meet shareholder expectations, the measurement system instructs employees how to create shareholder value. In this way, an effective performance measurement system can provide a company with a sustainable competitive advantage by providing a sound framework for making decisions.

Metric Selection

Designing an effective performance measurement system depends on having a thorough understanding of your company's business context. There is no standard system for measuring performance, so the objective is to choose from among the many available metrics those that provide the best fit with your organization and with the objectives of motivating and rewarding executives.

We will discuss performance metric selection in greater detail in Chapter 4, but as a starting point, companies will want to contemplate the following questions:

- What exactly do we want to measure?
- What measures most closely align with shareholder value?
- What measures fit the business strategy and work culture?
- What measures are most critical to success?
- To what extent do executives understand the measure?

What Do We Want to Measure?

As we have discussed, there are many different stages of value creation. Naturally, there are also many points along that value chain that could be measured. You could measure the specific activities that generate value. Or, you could look to important events to measure progress toward an end goal. You could also look at the end result—how much value has been created. For incentive purposes, executive performance is most commonly measured based on results—whether financial or market-related—that are closely associated with value creation.

Results are the most apparent indicators of performance, particularly to shareholders, and therefore cannot be overlooked. However, some companies may benefit from additionally linking rewards to the measurement of activities or events, as they can sometimes improve the line of sight between executive behaviors and results. For example, it is obvious that the contributions of the top *research and development* (R&D) executive in discovering new drugs or therapies are critical in generating shareholder value at a pharmaceutical company, but the executive's day-to-day activities may have little or no effect on total shareholder return. In fact, there may be a significant lag, years even, between the accomplishments of the R&D executive and the market response. In this case, metrics that capture activities, such as number of drug trials run, or events, such as completion of stage one research on a new drug, may be more effective indicators of executive performance, while still being closely aligned with the drivers of value creation.

What Measures Are Aligned with Value Creation?

Alignment is the key to both business performance and performance measurement. Whether talking about the chief operations officer, top information technology executive or top procurement executive, you want the behaviors of your executives to support the creation of shareholder value. And, because your end goal is to measure value creation, your performance measurement strategy should aim to capture those activities, events, and results that are the outcomes of this behavior. Close alignment between your strategy, executive behaviors, and measurement systems will better position your company for success by affecting a more engaged workforce.

Companies can identify metrics that are aligned with shareholder value through a combination of quantitative analysis and qualitative research. Analysis of the relationship between TSR and financial performance at your company and among your industry peers can provide valuable insight into the metrics mostly closely correlated with value creation. Discussions with shareholders can also reveal the metrics they focus on in assessing the company's current performance and gauging future prospects.

Another important consideration is your company's stage of development, since this can have a significant impact on shareholder expectations.

Specifically, for companies in the early stages of development, shareholders are less concerned with financial results and more concerned that the company meets key milestones that will position it for later success. As the company grows, shareholders begin to shift their attention to revenue as an early indicator that the strategy is translating into business success. Meanwhile, shareholders at more mature companies tend to focus on profitability as they begin to look for a more tangible return on their investment.

What Measures Fit the Business Strategy and Work Culture?

To develop a performance measurement system that supports your business strategy, you must have a thorough understanding of how your company intends to beat the competition. A department store makes money selling a variety of consumer products, but in order to succeed, it must present a compelling value proposition to the market and then capitalize on its competitive advantages to deliver on this strategy. Does the business intend to attract customers based on price, selection, customer service, convenience, or some combination of the above? If it intends to compete based on price, how will it secure its competitive advantage in being a low cost provider? How will it defend that position against other entrants into the market? The answers to questions like these will allow you to identify the drivers of value creation for your own business.

Value drivers fulfill several roles. They provide insight into opportunities for value creation and facilitate the ongoing strategy development process. They also help prioritize resource allocation and guide decision-making. At the highest level, value drivers include factors such as business design and organizational architecture, but the most effective value drivers are actionable leverage points that enhance the line of sight between shareholder value creation and operating behaviors at all levels in the organization. They may represent unique customer propositions or differentiated business processes that can significantly influence the company's value. Put simply, value drivers tell the story of the business strategy.

For example, a mature company, after reviewing several strategic alternatives, decided that they could reenergize growth and earnings by creating a start-up division to enter into a new market segment. Rather than focus on the return metrics used to measure performance under the existing incentive arrangements, the company measured performance for that division based on incremental free cash flow tied to strategic growth measures based on market penetration. Strategic measures were weighted more heavily in the first two years. Market penetration—the underlying value driver—would lead to increased free cash flow and free cash flow would drive long-term value creation.

There are other considerations in executing your strategic plan that may also come into play in your approach to performance measurement. For example, your business must be able to procure enough cash to cover its day-to-day financial obligations, and so the ability to secure short-term loans at an attractive rate is critical. If your company has had difficulty maintaining a line of credit in the current economic environment, then measures looked at closely by lenders (such as debt service coverage ratio) may become more important in measuring the contributions of finance executives.

The external environment may also determine the suitability of certain metrics. If your industry is heavily influenced by commodity prices, then absolute growth in revenues and profits will be driven largely by factors outside of the company's control. These metrics would therefore not provide a good fit with your business.

Finally, the work culture must be a primary consideration when assessing fit. Culture dictates the employee response to the selected metric and ultimately determines its ability to measure performance and drive shareholder value creation. A measure that effectively drives behaviors at one company may be poorly understood at another, or worse, may lead to unintended consequences such as employees manipulating results to their benefit. Before selecting any measure, a company must fairly assess its current culture, as well as its transformational capabilities should changes be required.

What Measures Are Most Important?

There are clearly many different dimensions to performance, yet incentive programs cannot be all-encompassing. The challenge is to focus on those factors that (1) are most closely aligned with value creation and (2) executives have the greatest ability to influence. Some companies find it helpful to describe these as *key success factors* (KSFs). The objective in identifying KSFs is to isolate those critical few factors that contribute disproportionally to success. Generally, the 80/20 rule can be applied to KSFs: They are responsible for 80 percent of a company's success, but are the outcome of only 20 percent of a company's efforts.

KSFs can be different across organizations, depending on business cycle, strategy, work culture, and other factors. Within the same organization they may vary by business unit or may change over time as the company matures or shifts strategic focus.

For example, a company had several business units in different market segments. One competed in markets where there was little room for pricing differences. This unit focused its KSFs on cost effectiveness. Another competed in markets with few constraints to growth. Their KSFs were focused on incremental growth in revenue. A third unit competed in markets that were well developed. Their KSFs were focused on providing innovate products that differentiated them from competitors. All of these businesses operated as part of a business portfolio governed by overarching corporate KSFs.

It is this variability that makes cookie-cutter solutions, such as Economic Value Added (EVA) or Balanced Scorecards, ineffective at many of the organizations in which they are implemented. In Chapter 5, we introduce the *unbalanced* scorecard as an alternative framework that allows companies to focus its performance measurement on those KSFs that best reflect current business priorities.

To What Extent Do Executives Understand the Measure?

The power of KSFs is to create focus on the most critical business outcomes. This underscores the importance of performance measurement not only in rewarding executives, but in motivating desired behaviors. A company's unique definition of performance is a potent communication message and the performance measurement system—particularly as it is linked to specific incentive remuneration programs—is a valuable communication tool.

Given its importance as a communication tool, workforce understanding must be considered in selecting performance metrics. If the incentive programs include too many metrics, the message may be diluted and executives will be confused as to how to focus their efforts. If the metrics are too complex or do not have a strong line of sight to day-to-day activities and decisions, executives will not know how to influence the measure and the incentive value will be lost.

In addition, executives must feel that they are connected to the metric in a meaningful way. If they do not feel empowered to act on opportunities that can generate the desired results, then the efficacy of the measure will be limited. This connection is often best forged through ongoing communication efforts and robust performance management processes.

Linkage

Determining the appropriate level to measure results is a key consideration when assessing performance. The answer will vary from company to company and depends primarily on how value is created in the business.

If the company has multiple business units, it will need to consider how much emphasis should be placed on business unit results versus company-wide performance. If the business units are highly independent, with few synergies across them, a greater emphasis on business unit outcomes may be appropriate. However, if value creation requires significant collaboration and cooperation across business units, a company may want to place greater emphasis on corporate results. Additionally, if customers can be serviced by a number of different business units, corporate results may promote greater cross selling. Ultimately, each company will need to determine where its value creating platforms exist and tailor its measurement approach to reflect this (see Exhibit 2.3).

Finally, linkage should reflect organizational design. For example, corporate executives should be held to corporate performance results, while business unit success would be measured at both the corporate and business unit level. This ensures proper line of sight between an executive's span of control and performance measurement processes. We discuss linkage further in Chapter 5.

Characteristics Favoring Use of Corporate Measures	Characteristics Favoring Use of Business Unit Measures
• Significant corporate management/ control of business units.	• Business unit develops own strategic plan with little corporate coordination.
• Business units interdependent because of shared resources/integrative strategies.	• Significant differences in business unit strategies/key success factors.
• Encourages collaboration among business units.	• Little interdependence: business units do not sell or transfer products to other company operations.
• Significant mobility of talent across business units.	• Little mobility of talent across business units.
• Supports one-company culture.	
	• Need to support strong business unit cultures/values.

Exhibit 2.3   Focus on Corporate versus Business Unit Measures
SOURCE: Mercer.

Goal Setting

Determining the right measures to capture performance is important, but value creation cannot be accurately assessed if goals are not set properly. There are various approaches for translating measures into specific goals, but ideally, the goal setting process will be informed by internal considerations, such as incremental improvement over the prior period and internal budgets, as well as external context, such as macroeconomic indicators, peer historical and expected performance, and shareholder expectations.

A company will also need to determine if goals should be set in absolute or relative terms. Absolute internal goals enable a company to recognize both internal factors and external context. A clearly defined internal goal can help rally executives and employees around a common objective and enables the company to track and report on progress over time, whereas relative goals can be more difficult to communicate.

On the other hand, an external goal tied to an industry benchmark eliminates the need to set hard targets and captures any market or industry shifts in the relative measurement process. However, implementation can be a challenge; peer data are not always available to make meaningful and timely assessments of performance, and apples-to-apples comparisons of financial results across companies can sometimes be difficult depending on the metric.

Like other aspects of the performance measurement system, the goal-setting approach must reflect a company's unique business context, as well as external conditions that can impact performance. For example, if your company operates in a highly cyclical industry, targets set based on improvement over the prior year's financial results would not provide much insight into real performance. In down cycles, performance would automatically appear poor, while in boom cycles it may unjustly appear strong. Relative performance measurement, where performance is judged against peers subject to the same environmental influences, would likely be more accurate in capturing real performance in this situation.

The most robust performance measurement systems capture a wide variety of perspectives, internal and external, relative and absolute. We discuss this and many other considerations for target setting in Chapter 7.

Time Horizon

One reason that narrow approaches to performance measurement tend to fail is that the business outcomes that arise from executive actions manifest in different ways over time. Leadership decisions, such as establishing the business strategy, begin the value creation process and are followed by operational execution of critical strategic initiatives. The full effects of these activities may not show up on the company's financial results for months, or even years. The market response can lag even further behind.

Given this reality, most companies aim to measure and reward performance over multiple, overlapping time periods. Traditionally, for-profit companies have rewarded executives annually for the achievement of strategic and financial goals and have used equity to reward market performance over a longer time period. In recent years, more and more companies have adopted long-term incentive plans that link rewards to the achievement of financial goals as well as absolute stock price.

In designing the annual incentive plan, companies should emphasize the near-term financial and strategic priorities of the business. The metrics used to measure performance should be derived from the business strategy and should reflect the value drivers that contribute to long-term shareholder value creation. They may include both quantitative financial metrics, as well as more qualitative strategic goals that will position the business for future performance. For example, if a company's business strategy hinges on capturing market share in an emerging product market, the short-term incentive plan should include metrics related to the execution of this initiative. Financial metrics could include revenue growth attributable to the new product, while strategic metrics might include acquiring a well-positioned competitor or setting up new distribution channels.

Long-term incentive plans typically focus more directly on shareholder value creation. Equity-based plans reward executives for increases in share price and dividends, while performance-based plans condition awards on the achievement of specified goals. Relative TSR is a common metric in long-term incentive plans, as it can better qualify absolute TSR results by comparing them against the TSR of similarly positioned peers.

Financial measures are also becoming more prevalent in long-term incentive plans. Return measures, such as return on assets or return on invested capital, are particularly well suited to long-term incentive programs since they capture how well a company has leveraged its assets to generate value over time. Economic metrics, such as total business return and cash flow return on investment, are also well suited to long-term incentive plans since they approximate value creation from an internal business perspective. These metrics are more complex, but also more accurate than return metrics because they capture both the level and magnitude of returns.

Short-term and long-term incentive plans should reinforce one another. Performance captured in the short-term plan should drive the results that determine long-term incentives. This enables the company to send a clear and consistent message to executives about performance, while not rewarding executives more than once for the same results.

In addition, the balance between short- and long-term focus should reflect each company's unique value creation proposition. In industries that rely heavily on research and development to generate value, such as aerospace or biotechnology, value creation may occur over years or

The Respective Roles of Company ABC's Reward Programs (Example)

	What are the organization's priorities and business goals?				How are these priorities/goals reflected over different time frames?			How are accountability and line of site reinforced and at what levels?			On what basis is performance assessed?	
	Growth	Profitability	Capital Efficiency and Returns	Shareholder Value Growth (TSR)	Near-term	Mid-term	Long-term	Corporate	Group	Individual	Relative	Absolute
Base salary	★	★								★		A
Annual bonus		★			▮			★	★	★		A
Performance shares			★	★		▮		★			R	
Stock options				★			▮	★				A

Exhibit 2.4   Incentive Framework

SOURCE: Mercer.

even decades, whereas the value creation cycle may be significantly shorter in other industries, like media. Whatever the emphasis, the short-term incentive plan should not offer excessive rewards for risk-taking, and opportunities afforded through the long-term incentive plan should be sufficient enough to discourage executives from inflating short-term results through actions that hurt the long-term viability of the company.

While many companies design their remuneration plans independently, a better approach is to design an overarching rewards framework that captures shareholder value creation at various stages in time (Exhibit 2.4). This framework, which would ideally identify measurement parameters like metrics, linkage, time horizon and target setting approach, can then be translated into specific remuneration elements and incentive plan designs. This holistic approach ensures a high degree of balance in the performance measurement system, as well as top-down alignment within the organization.

Striking the Right Balance

When it comes to defining performance, there are many competing interests, alternative perspectives and varying objectives that make it a very gray area indeed. The challenge is to strike the right balance in decision making. Companies must find the proper balance between risk and reward, short-term and long-term orientation, and financial and strategic goals. This requires separating accounting results from economic performance, and understanding how business results drive market reactions.

Above all, companies must strive to pay for *real* performance—not just *good* performance. Companies should not overpay just because performance seems good. If results are not sustainable or do not truly drive shareholder value creation, the performance is more an illusion than a reality.

At the same time, companies sometimes have to make the difficult decision to reward executives when performance appears to be down. There is no magic number that can be relied on to capture value creation—not TSR or any other single factor. Performance is the culmination of a wide variety of factors and only a comprehensive analysis of results will lead you to the right answer.

Companies need a clear rationale to defend doing what is required. This book provides the tools necessary to design incentive programs that hone in on real performance results. In addition, we identify those challenges that cannot be addressed through plan design in order to help companies overcome obstacles by employing a well-informed decision-making process that recognizes the many dimensions of performance.

Chapter 3

Back to Basics

An Introduction to Mercer's Performance Framework

The creation of shareholder value is the ultimate goal for any company. As such, managing your organization for value creation can be a powerful way to enhance business performance. This management approach, often referred to as *managing for value,* is essentially an organizational mind-set that aligns day-to-day activities and decisions with the objective of increasing shareholder value.

A carefully designed performance measurement system provides the necessary language for addressing value management at all levels of the organization. Indeed, it is the foundation on which a managing-for-value mind-set grows and flourishes. By identifying those factors that drive value creation, it enables a company to bring organizational processes—such as information sharing, decision making, and reward determination—into alignment with a single goal.

To understand how this mind-set can be instilled through the performance measurement system and reinforced by executive remuneration and broader rewards programs, we must go back to the basics and investigate how organizations create value. Among for-profit companies, we find that economic value aligns with external shareholder value over time, so the search for the specific behaviors that drive value creation—as well as the metrics that most accurately capture the outcomes of these behaviors—must begin with a thorough understanding of what economic value is.

With the interrelated goals of driving economic value creation and verifying internal results based on external shareholder experience, Mercer has developed an adaptable framework for performance measurement design. While we believe strongly that every company is unique and requires a customized approach to value management, there are some general principles that should be adhered to. Most importantly, effective performance measurement systems must recognize four essential components of value creation: growth, profits, returns, and shareholder experience. In this chapter, we explore how companies can determine the trade-offs between the various dimensions of performance to design a comprehensive measurement system tailored to their own unique business and cultural context.

Why Manage for Shareholder Value

Focusing on shareholder value creation has multiple advantages, both from a process, or decision-making, perspective, as well as from a fiduciary standpoint. A shareholder-driven mind-set provides:

- *Clarity on the enterprise objective.* All stakeholders, including employees, need to understand why the business exists. Without a shared understanding of this most fundamental concept, people will work in a manner that is disjointed or even counterproductive.
- *A common language for getting things done.* A managing-for-value mind-set provides a vocabulary that enables management to communicate the business strategy and unite employees behind a common purpose.

- *Ability to evaluate trade-offs in resource allocation.* Stakeholders sometimes have competing interests and will advocate that resources be distributed in a way that benefits them. A singular, overriding goal provides an objective basis for judging alternative opportunities for investment.
- *A roadmap for the future.* A common definition of success empowers employees to identify, evaluate, and pursue new business opportunities that are aligned with the objective of value creation.
- *Alignment of key processes.* The business signals its priorities through many different activities, including remuneration and career decisions, internal and external communication, and performance management processes. When all of these processes are embedded in a value management mind-set, the message to employees is consistent and powerful.

Systems Thinking

A managing-for-value mind-set enables the organization to function in a coordinated manner by ensuring all constituents are focused on a singular goal—shareholder value creation. It is a way of thinking, a guiding philosophy.

The performance measurement system helps make this philosophy more tangible for employees of the company. It can be thought of as a tool for translating the value creation strategy into actionable goals. In addition to establishing goals, the performance measurement system enables a company to determine accountability, track results, and diagnose business outcomes (see Exhibit 3.1). All of these activities feed back to the drivers of shareholder value, resulting in a dynamic system that allows companies to continually validate the significance of the metrics chosen to measure performance.

While this book focuses on performance outcomes as a basis for rewarding executives, performance measurement is embedded in a number of corporate processes. Different business processes may require different measurement approaches or different subsets of the portfolio of measures you select for rewarding executives. Some processes that rely on the performance measurement system include the allocation of

Exhibit 3.1   Performance Measurement Cycle
SOURCE: Mercer.

capital, financial reporting, communication with internal and external audiences, budgeting activities, and performance management.

As we have discussed, the objective around which everything else revolves—the reason specific metrics are chosen to measure specific business processes—is the creation of shareholder value. Exhibit 3.2 shows the relationships between some key corporate processes and the metrics that focus them on this overriding objective. In this example, six processes have been shown to contribute to shareholder value, and a range of related metrics have been designated to track and verify the success of the company's efforts to support activities in these areas.

Many metrics are useful for several or all of the purposes identified, but some are more targeted than others when it comes to particular business functions. For example, the incentive remuneration strategy, in order to support the objective of creating shareholder value, focuses on share price appreciation, earnings before interest and taxes, and free cash flow. The process of allocating capital, on the other hand, relies on an analysis of economic profit and discounted cash flow.

While you do not need *consistency* of measures across various business processes, you do need *alignment*. If measures are not aligned, they will send competing signals to employees, which will quickly undermine the value management mind-set.

A holistic approach to performance measurement design ensures that corporate processes are integrated and designed to reinforce one

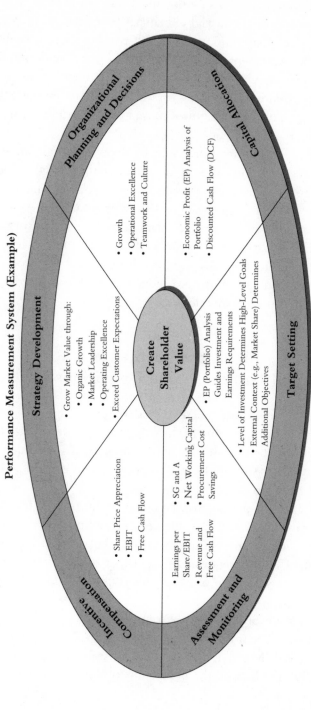

Performance Measurement System (Example)

Organizational Planning and Decisions

Capital Allocation

Strategy Development

- Growth
- Operational Excellence
- Teamwork and Culture

- Economic Profit (EP) Analysis of Portfolio
- Discounted Cash Flow (DCF)

- Grow Market Value through:
  - Organic Growth
  - Market Leadership
  - Operating Excellence
- Exceed Customer Expectations

Create Shareholder Value

- EP (Portfolio) Analysis Guides Investment and Earnings Requirements

- Level of Investment Determines High-Level Goals
- External Context (e.g., Market Share) Determines Additional Objectives

Target Setting

- Share Price Appreciation
- EBIT
- Free Cash Flow

- SG and A
- Net Working Capital
- Procurement Cost Savings

- Earnings per Share/EBIT
- Revenue and Free Cash Flow

Incentive Compensation

Assessment and Monitoring

Exhibit 3.2 Key Business Processes and the Metrics Used to Gauge Performance in Each Area

SOURCE: Mercer.

another. For example, you can only use a chosen metric to determine incentive awards if the right financial processes are in place to track the measure. Communication is also paramount to an effective performance measurement system. Executives must understand the measurement system, what it will be used for, and how it links to their day-to-day contributions in order for the system to properly guide decision-making. This often requires substantial education up-front, as well as ongoing reinforcement.

In designing a comprehensive performance measurement system like the one outlined thus far, it is important at the outset to identify the business drivers that are most important in your company. As we see in Chapter 4, identifying the value drivers in your business requires the synthesis of both qualitative and quantitative inputs. Statistical analysis of historical performance, current performance, and projections of future performance are the hard numbers that figure in this process, but individual experience, intuition, and judgment are the final arbiters of which drivers and metrics are selected.

Alignment of Internal and External Value Definitions

As we discussed in Chapter 2, shareholder value is created through increases in the enterprise value of the company. In order to develop an integrated performance measurement system aligned with value creation, we must further explore how enterprise value is created and what factors influence it most significantly.

From an external perspective, enterprise value equals the market value of a company's equity (i.e., market capitalization or the number of shares outstanding times share price) plus the value of outstanding debt. The market value of equity can be further broken down into two components: the book value of equity plus "market value added" (see Exhibit 3.3).

The book value of equity is the capital invested in the enterprise by shareholders as recorded on the company's accounting statement. *Market value added* (MVA) is the premium shareholders assign to the enterprise above and beyond the book value of their investment.

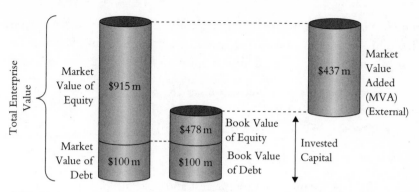

Exhibit 3.3 Components of Enterprise Value (External Perspective)
Source: Mercer.

Since the book value of equity is static, MVA is the primary component that can be altered to drive shareholder value creation. Thus, management's objective must be to grow MVA over time. As suggested in Chapter 2, MVA reflects a wide range of factors, including market and industry influences, current performance, expectations for future performance and intangibles associated with the business. The key to implementing a value management mind-set is to identify those factors that impact MVA and manage them in a way that maximizes the premium applied by the public market.

Our definition of market value reflects two sources of capital available to companies: equity and debt. *Equity capital* is money provided by investors and requires a minimum rate of return that varies across companies and over time. This *required rate of return,* or *cost of equity* (K_e), depends on several market factors, including the current risk-free rate and a company's degree of portfolio risk. Providers of debt capital agree to a specified rate of return, known as the interest rate, which is to be paid back over time along with the principal. Because interest rates are established up front as a condition of the loan, required returns are met through ongoing interest payments. As a result, our discussion of value creation can focus on the extent to which returns based on net income (i.e., income after *interest* and taxes) exceeds equity investor expectations.

From an internal or "economic" value perspective, the value of equity can be derived from the discounted sum of future economic profits. Future streams of economic profit (EP) are discounted to put the value in today's dollars. EP is defined by returns in excess of the cost of equity and can be calculated as follows:

Economic profit = Net income—(K_e × Market value of equity)
Net income = EBIT − Interest paid − Taxes
$K_e = R_f + (\beta$ × Market risk premium$)^1$

where

EBIT = Earnings before interest and taxes
R_f = Risk free rate
β = Beta

In other words, economic profit represents the returns available to investors of the business after paying for the costs of operating the business (e.g., cost of goods sold, selling, general and administrative costs, interest, taxes) *and* meeting the opportunity cost to investors. Discounted economic profit can be used as an internal proxy for market value added (see Exhibit 3.4) and EP generation can be used to focus management efforts on controllable business results.

At any single point in time, economic value may differ from market value added. If investors see greater opportunities for the company than management has incorporated into its strategic plan, market value added (external) may exceed economic value (internal). On the other hand, if investors question the credibility of management's forecasts or see too much risk in the current business strategy, external valuations may fall short of economic estimates. Over time, however, economic value should converge with external shareholder value creation.

---

[1]The cost of equity (K_e) is the minimum return required for an investor to be indifferent between this investment and a risk-free environment. It can be estimated by adding the risk-free rate to the product of a company's beta (β) and the market risk premium. Risk-free rate is the rate of return guaranteed through government bonds and can be estimated by looking at the rate of return on a 10-year U.S. Treasury bill. Beta is an estimate of a company's portfolio risk; the higher the beta, the greater the risk which cannot be mitigated through a diversified approach to investing. Market risk premium is the premium required for equity investments with a Beta of 1, and although this figure is subject to much debate, it is generally accepted to be approximately 5 percent based on historical equity returns.

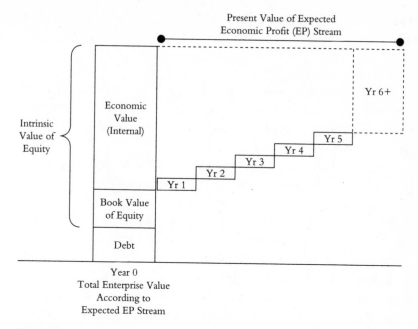

Exhibit 3.4 Components of Enterprise Value (Internal Perspective)
Source: Mercer.

Value Creation Demystified

Given that economic value aligns with external market value over time, an analysis of EP provides important messages regarding value creation in your business:

- If EP is > 0, the company is exceeding investors' minimum expectations (return on equity > cost of equity) and value is being created.
- If EP < 0, the company is returning less than investors' minimum expectations (return on equity < cost of equity) and value is being destroyed.

If economic profit is less than zero, your company's most urgent priority must be to get economic profit above zero before it destroys any more value. If economic profit is greater than zero, your company's highest priorities will be to protect this level of profitability and to find ways to grow the enterprise.

There are four fundamental ways to execute on these priorities and generate value in any business:

1. *Grow economically profitable parts of the business and/or undertake new business ventures that promise economic profitability.* This could mean entering new markets with a proven product or service, expanding relationships with profitable customers, or entering new product or service markets.
2. *Improve economic cost structures or margins.* Ways to accomplish this include lowering overhead costs, increasing operational efficiencies, or expanding operations to better capitalize on economies of scale.
3. *Exit unprofitable businesses.* Projects that do not have a high probability of generating positive economic profit on their own and are not essential to value creation in other parts of the business should be abandoned in favor of greener pastures.
4. *Reduce the investment risks associated with the business.* By reducing risks relative to competitors, companies may be able to lower the minimum returns required by investors, resulting in a lower threshold to generate positive economic profit.

Fostering a managing-for-value mind-set and developing a credible performance measurement system to facilitate and reward value creation requires understanding the drivers of performance, which will undoubtedly be embedded in one or more of these approaches to value creation.

Balancing Growth and Returns

The four avenues to value creation outlined in the previous section underpin the importance of balancing the sometimes competing objectives of growing the business and maximizing returns. It is impossible to generate shareholder value by expanding the business if the cost structures are not in place or risks are not appropriately managed so as to allow for the generation of positive EP in the first place. In fact, growing the business when EP is negative simply results in the destruction of more value.

On the other hand, it is difficult to "shrink" your way to success by focusing solely on returns. Strong returns must be leveraged through growth to generate greater amounts of EP and affect meaningful increases in external shareholder valuations.

To illustrate this point, consider the range of possible economic profit results for a company given varying levels of returns and growth as detailed in Exhibit 3.5. If returns do not exceed the cost of capital, value will be destroyed rather than created (and in greater amounts under higher-growth scenarios). When returns exceed the cost of capital, however, growth in the business will generate more meaningful increases in EP. Clearly, companies benefit from improvements in both returns and revenue to a greater extent than if management were to focus on one factor to the exclusion of the other.

Mercer's research provides further evidence of the advantage that results from both improving returns and growing the business. As shown in Exhibit 3.6, companies that have both upper quartile returns and upper quartile levels of revenue growth deliver significantly higher levels of shareholder return, as captured by external measures like total

Economic Profit ($M) under Various Growth and Return Scenarios[a]

Return on Invested Capital

Revenue Growth	4%	6%	8%	10%	12%	14%
−20%	−$6.4	−$3.2	$0.0	$3.2	$6.4	$9.6
−10%	−$7.2	−$3.6	$0.0	$3.6	$7.2	$10.8
0%	−$8.0	−$4.0	$0.0	$4.0	$8.0	$12.0
10%	−$8.8	−$4.4	$0.0	$4.4	$8.8	$13.2
20%	−$9.6	−$4.8	$0.0	$4.8	$9.6	$14.4
30%	−$10.4	−$5.2	$0.0	$5.2	$10.4	$15.6
40%	−$11.2	−$5.6	$0.0	$5.6	$11.2	$16.8
50%	−$12.0	−$6.0	$0.0	$6.0	$12.0	$18.0
60%	−$12.8	−$6.4	$0.0	$6.4	$12.8	$19.2

Value Destroyed   Value Created

[a]Assumes starting revenues of $200 million and weighted average cost of capital of 8%.

Exhibit 3.5 Matrix Comparing EP Levels under Various Growth and Return Scenarios

SOURCE: Mercer.

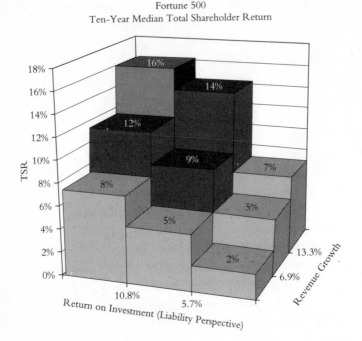

Exhibit 3.6   Relationship between Revenue Growth, ROI, and TSR
Source: Mercer.

shareholder return, than companies that do poorly on one or both measures. Furthermore, companies with moderately strong returns and growth tend to outperform companies that perform well in one area but are weak in the other.

Mercer's Performance Measurement Framework

Growth measures indicate how well a company is leveraging its business strategy to expand the business. Profitability measures describe the extent to which revenues exceed the direct and indirect costs associated with generating those revenues. Return measures compare profit levels to the amount of capital invested in the business. Finally, the end result of value creation is directly measured by shareholder-related metrics.

Each of these dimensions of performance is a critical component in the chain of value creation (see Exhibit 3.7). The first three—growth,

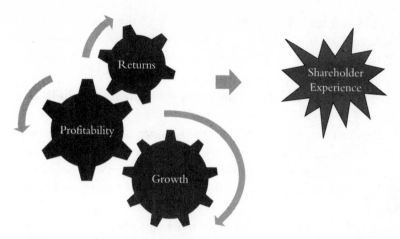

Exhibit 3.7   Dimensions of Performance
SOURCE: Mercer.

profits, and returns—contribute directly to the creation of economic value. The latter, shareholder experience, is the manifestation of performance on the first three dimensions as perceived by the public market.

Mercer's performance measurement framework is founded on the belief that each of these dimensions must be captured in the performance measurement system in order to drive value creation. However, this is not to say that every company should use the exact same metrics. There is an infinite universe of potential metrics that could be used to capture these aspects of performance, ranging the simplest measures like volume and revenue to more complex economic concepts such as *cash flow return on investment* (CFROI) and *total business return* (TBR)[2]. Each company needs to select those metrics that most accurately capture growth, profitability, returns, and shareholder experience at their own organization and then customize the metrics to fit the company's unique business and organizational context.

We discuss specific strategies for approaching metric selection in the next chapter, but let us begin by reviewing some of the more common

---

[2]CFROI is an approximate of the average internal rate of return earned by a company on all its operating assets. TBR is a forward-looking measurement of CFROI.

metrics used to measure performance, including their advantages and limitations. Among the many metrics available, financial metrics are the most common because they are objective, quantifiable, and relatively easy to compare across competing businesses.

Revenue is an excellent measure of top-line growth. It tells us how much money the company has received for the goods and services it provides, and is a function of volume (the number of units, transactions, or services provided to customers) and price (the cost per unit, transaction, or service). Yet, revenue cannot tell you anything about how much money the company is earning or the capital required to generate the revenue.

Earnings-based measures provide more information, since they match up revenues with the expenses associated with the generating the revenue. Profit margins (earnings divided by revenue) indicate a company's degree of profitability, while absolute earnings-based measures, such as net income or earnings per share, reflect the magnitude of profits. Still, profitability measures ignore the amount of capital used in the business.

Return measures, such as *return on equity* (ROE) or *return on invested capital* (ROIC), enable more accurate comparisons of performance results by addressing capital intensity. As shown in Exhibit 3.8, a company's level of capital investments is a crucial component to understanding performance results.

Yet return measures have limitations as well. They can potentially distort the amount of capital used by the business since returns calculated using the information reported in accounting statements rely on the initial purchase price and GAAP-based depreciation, rather than the value of assets today. Return measures also fail to recognize the cost of obtaining this capital through banks or investors.

Each of the concerns identified so far can be addressed by adding more information to the metric or by making adjustments to account for potential distortions. These actions usually improve the accuracy of the metric in capturing the drivers of shareholder value creation, but also increase the complexity of the metric (see Exhibit 3.9).

The trade-off between accuracy and complexity is an important consideration for every company, as a chosen measure can only be effective in so far as it is understood by those who are expected

	High-Intensity Company	Low-Intensity Company
Revenue	$2,400	$2,000
Expenses	$2,000	$1,700
Earnings	$400	$300
Capital	$4,000	$1,500
Return on Capital	**10%**	**20%**

Exhibit 3.8   Impact of Capital Intensity on Performance Assessment
SOURCE: Mercer.

to apply it as part of their day-to-day decision-making process. If the measurement system is too complex, executives may not understand how their behaviors are linked to the performance metric without significant up-front education and ongoing reinforcement through regular communication and appropriate reporting systems.

The right balance between accuracy and complexity depends on the existing business strategy and work culture, as well as the resources that can be devoted to implementing and supporting the measurement system over time. Companies with very simple business models and business-minded talent may find that they can capture the internal dimensions of performance effectively using an economic-based measure. If the value creation process is straightforward, there will be strong line of sight between executives' day-to-day activities and the generation of economic value. In addition, the amount of effort required to instill a value-management mind-set may be relatively small.

On the other hand, a complex organization with many diverse business units may find it more challenging to measure and manage executive performance by utilizing a corporate-wide economic measure. A more flexible performance measurement approach utilizing a combination of distinct growth, profitability, and return metrics might be more suitable since it would enable the customization of the performance measures or weightings to reflect varying stages of maturity or different strategic priorities among various parts of the business. For example, a mature business unit might place greater weight on profitability and return metrics, while an emerging business unit might focus

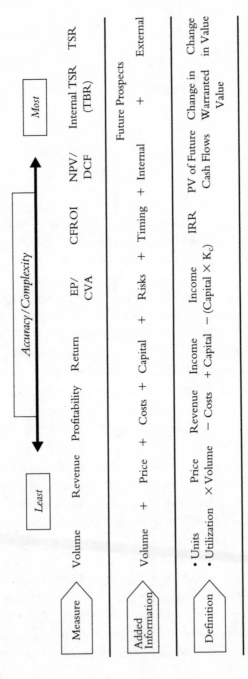

Exhibit 3.9. Trade–Off between Accuracy and Complexity in Measure Selection

Source: Mercer.

more heavily on growth. Executives at both business units could be tied to shareholder experience through the use of equity-based incentive vehicles.

Just as the types of metrics used to capture growth, profitability, returns, and shareholder experience vary from company to company, so too may the definition of performance metric. For example, the definition of ROIC at a capital intensive manufacturing business may vary significantly from the way the same metric is defined at a retail chain. The manufacturing company may make adjustments to the capital base to recognize that fact that equipment depreciates at a faster or slower rate than is captured through GAAP-based accounting, while the retail chain may incorporate capitalized leases (which, unlike property purchased outright, are not reflected on the balance sheet) into their definition of invested capital.

The example in the previous paragraph illustrates the importance of scrutinizing the definition of performance metrics to ensure that they appropriately reflect individual business circumstances. If generic definitions are applied blindly, your company runs the risk of measuring the wrong thing. On the other hand, if metric adjustments are too numerous or complicated, the measure may not be understood by participants or could lose its relevance, especially when comparing performance against competitors. In determining the best definition of a metric, companies need to ask whether the standard definition (e.g., accounting-based measures) meets the needs of the measurement system or if adjustments would make it a more relevant decision-making tool. Some questions to consider include:

- Will the adjustment have a material impact on results?
- Is the adjustment meaningful to employees?
- Is the adjustment consistent with other metrics/adjustments in the wider performance measurement system?
- Will the adjustment reinforce the desired behavior?
- Is there adequate information available to make the adjustment?
- If performance is measured on a relative basis, will the adjustment allow for an apples-to-apples comparison against peers?
- Is the added complexity worth the gain?

The last point is crucial. Just as there are trade-offs between accuracy and complexity in metric selection, there are trade-offs between accuracy and complexity in defining performance measures. Any adjustments to standard metric definitions must warrant the time and effort required not only in collecting the required information and calculating results, but in explaining the metric to both executives and shareholders.

Case Study: Performance Measurement at Manufacture Co.

To get an idea for how a company might go about designing a performance measurement plan that captures the multiple dimensions of performance, let us consider a real-life example. Manufacture Co. is a midsize multinational corporation that designs and manufactures a low-tech industrial product. After in-depth analysis of Manufacture Co.'s industry financial results, three key observations were made and several implications for the company's performance measurement system were identified, as shown in Exhibit 3.10.

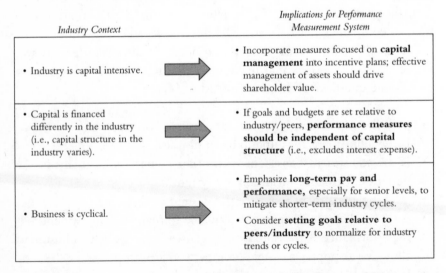

Industry Context	Implications for Performance Measurement System
• Industry is capital intensive.	• Incorporate measures focused on **capital management** into incentive plans; effective management of assets should drive shareholder value.
• Capital is financed differently in the industry (i.e., capital structure in the industry varies).	• If goals and budgets are set relative to industry/peers, **performance measures should be independent of capital structure** (i.e., excludes interest expense).
• Business is cyclical.	• Emphasize **long-term pay and performance,** especially for senior levels, to mitigate shorter-term industry cycles. • Consider **setting goals relative to peers/industry** to normalize for industry trends or cycles.

Exhibit 3.10   Industry Context and Implications for Performance Measurement
SOURCE: Mercer.

In addition to considering its industry context, Manufacture Co. also considered what implications the company's business strategy should have for the measurement system. In particular, Manufacturing Co. identified three strategic priorities that it expected to drive shareholder value in the near future, as shown in Exhibit 3.11.

Based on these findings, Manufacture Co. developed a proposed measurement approach around which it designed an executive incentive program shown in Exhibit 3.12. The incentive program captures all four of the dimensions outlined in Mercer's performance measurement framework.

The company decided that it would focus on profitability in measuring short-term performance. To encourage continual improvement, the profitability measure would be evaluated on a year-over-year basis. In addition, the annual incentive plan would include strategic objectives that focused on expanding the business through the identification and integration of profitable acquisitions in target geographies.

A return measure was selected for use in the long-term plan. Return measures are generally better suited for evaluating long-term

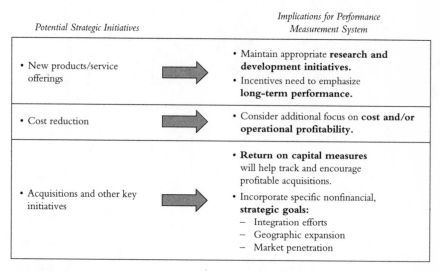

Potential Strategic Initiatives	*Implications for Performance Measurement System*
• New products/service offerings	• Maintain appropriate **research and development initiatives.** • Incentives need to emphasize **long-term performance.**
• Cost reduction	• Consider additional focus on **cost and/or operational profitability.**

• Acquisitions and other key initiatives	• **Return on capital measures** will help track and encourage profitable acquisitions.
	• Incorporate specific nonfinancial, **strategic goals:**
	  − Integration efforts
	  − Geographic expansion
	  − Market penetration

Exhibit 3.11   Strategic Context and Implications for Performance Measurement

SOURCE: Mercer.

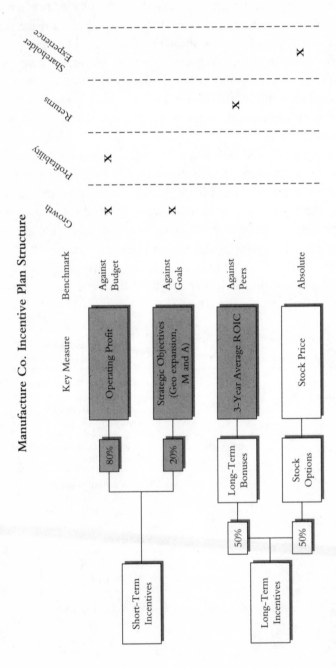

Exhibit 3.12   Manufacture Co. Incentive Plan Structure

SOURCE: Mercer.

performance, because it is not always possible (or desirable) to manage capital over an annual time period. For example, when investing capital to acquire a new business, the assets you purchase immediately hit the balance sheet even though you may not realize the full return on the investment (e.g., from integrating administrative functions, leveraging product synergies, or cross-selling to customers) for some time. This timing mismatch can be more appropriately managed and rewarded over multiple years. Adjustments to the metric definition—such as gradually incorporating acquisitions that exceed a certain size over a longer time period—might also be appropriate to accurately gauge performance results.

In addition, Manufacture Co. determined that a portion of the long-term incentive opportunity would be delivered through stock options. Stock options more directly reward increases in stock price and provide clear alignment with shareholder interests. By using a variety of metrics to evaluate results over the short- and long-term, Manufacture Co. takes a more holistic view of performance and avoids rewarding or penalizing participants more than once for performance against the same goals.

One Size Doesn't Fit All

As the experience at Manufacture Co. clearly demonstrates, an off-the-shelf solution will never be as effective as one that has been custom designed to reflect the external and strategic context of the business. Companies looking to promote a value management mind-set must tackle the challenge of performance measurement in a manner that captures the critical dimensions of performance (growth, profits, returns, and shareholder experience), while at the same time recognizing the unique strategic and cultural imperatives of the business.

In the next chapter, we give you the tools to begin putting this concept into practice. We also explore a series of quantitative and qualitative inputs that can help you to select the right performance metrics for your company—metrics that are closely aligned with value creation *and* provide a good fit with the business and organizational context.

Chapter 4

Trust, but Verify

Bringing Defensibility to Performance Metric Selection

L ike a fingerprint, every business is unique. It is a one-of-a-kind combination of elements: size, business model, organizational design, products, services, lifecycle stage, and management processes—not to mention a unique and constantly evolving mix of human capital. Success rests on keeping these elements and related processes working together smoothly in focused pursuit of your company's strategic goals. To help keep track of how well these elements are working, and to reward the people who are developing and executing the business strategy, you have to select the right performance metrics.

Selecting and prioritizing these metrics is not a simple task. There is no magic formula that crunches the numbers and spits out an answer. In the end, the selection of performance metrics requires a balanced process—a reasoned judgment based on facts, research, experience, and instinct.

It does not, however, have to be a guessing game. There are a wide range of inputs available to help you identify those metrics that will most effectively support shareholder value creation at your organization. In this chapter, we explore some of the tools that can help point you in the right direction and bring greater defensibility to the metric selection process.

Metric Selection in a Nutshell

In Chapter 3 we introduced a wide range of potential measures that companies can use to evaluate executive performance, ranging from simple metrics such as volume and revenue to more complex measures of intrinsic value creation such as economic profit. To trim that list down to the most applicable measures for your organization, you must balance consideration of your company's internal business context with other factors, such as alignment with shareholder experience and design practicality. Exhibit 4.1 lays out the significant elements that play a part in making those choices.

A company's internal business context determines how well particular metrics "fit" with the organization. Some metrics are designed to capture the dynamics of a specific industry, such as membership growth or patient satisfaction within the health care industry, or the differential between actual and breakeven load factors among airline companies. Industry economics can also influence how a measure is defined or used, such as emphasizing relative performance metrics in highly cyclical or commodity-driven industries where absolute goals can quickly become obsolete.

The best metrics also fit well with the company, recognizing factors such as organizational design, corporate culture, and management decision-making processes. For example, team-based metrics are much more successful at motivating and rewarding performance in a highly collaborative environment, while individual metrics are generally more effective in a culture that stresses personal accountability. Another company-specific consideration is the complexity of the business. Companies with diversified business operations require metrics that are customizable to the varying needs of different business units.

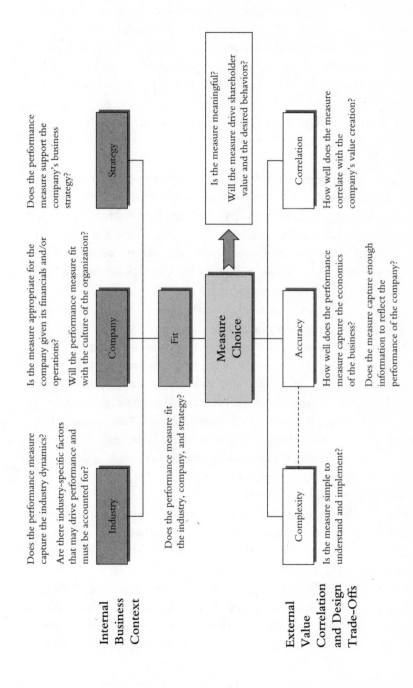

Exhibit 4.1   Decision Process for Choosing Performance Measures

Most importantly, the selected metrics must be embedded in the company's business strategy. A high-end jewelry retailer whose competitive advantage lies in providing superior products and customer service may choose to monitor customer-focused metrics, such as brand awareness or in-store customer conversion rates, whereas a discount retailer that competes primarily on price would be more interested in efficiency or margin-related measures, such as revenue per square foot or payroll cost as a percent of sales. Business stage is also important; as a company matures and its strategy evolves, the metrics used to the gauge performance should gradually shift in emphasis from growth to profitability and returns.

Fit with your company's internal business context determines how meaningful a measure is to your business. Yet not all measures that are meaningful to your organization will be equally effective in driving value creation or influencing employee behaviors. Companies must also test the strength of the relationship between potential measures and shareholder experience and evaluate design trade-offs, such as the appropriate balance between accuracy and complexity.

There are several tools available to assess the relationship between financial metrics and shareholder value creation. Regression analysis quantifies the correlation between external shareholder metrics, such as *total shareholder return* (TSR), and selected financial measures by analyzing changes over time. Other quantitative analyses, such as Performance Sensitivity Analysis®, provide insight into the relative importance of internal versus external measures of value creation. Value driver analysis can be used to break down key performance indicators into smaller, behavior-based components that provide enhanced line of sight to individual performance. We cover these and other informative analyses in detail later in the chapter.

There are also practical trade-offs between accuracy and complexity that must be taken into consideration. As discussed in Chapter 3, the more complex the measure, the more likely it is to capture the full range of elements that influence value creation. Yet, complex measures can sometimes be difficult to track and more often can pose challenges in educating and communicating with stakeholders. If employees do not understand the measures being used to assess performance, the ability of the measurement system to influence decision-making will be limited.

Given all of the factors that must be taken into account when selecting performance metrics, it is helpful to consider exactly what you need your performance measurement system to do. For incentive-based remuneration, metrics need to signal exactly "for what" companies are willing to pay executives. Beyond rewards, the metrics must support an array of business needs, such as establishing the criteria for capital investments, evaluating strategic alternatives, or providing a foundation for shareholder communications. By defining the specific objectives of your measurement system up-front, you can help establish parameters for the system design—including the proper balance between accuracy and complexity.

Market Research: A Limited, but Informative Tool

An effective measurement system can be tailored to fit your company's unique needs—from that point on it becomes your *fingerprint*. This does not mean that you need to invent new metrics to recognize your company's unique virtues and idiosyncrasies. On the contrary, it is helpful and preferable to select from a suite of metrics that are well-established measures of performance.

Conventional metrics are often easier to communicate to shareholders and executives for they are likely to be familiar with them as a measure of business performance. Conventional metrics may also be more effective at guiding employee decision making since goals that are clearly understood are, by extension, more actionable. Furthermore, standardized metrics allow for more accurate comparisons of your company's performance against peers, which can go a long way toward enhancing the credibility of executive remuneration programs, particularly in the eyes of shareholders.

A simple way to jumpstart the metric selection process is to use market research to understand what measures are commonly used to track performance in your industry and related sectors. More specifically, your research should answer three questions:

1. What measures are other companies in the industry and related sectors using?

2. What measures are commonly used by analysts and by other external sources to evaluate your company, your peers, and similar businesses?

3. What measures are simple and familiar enough to be understood by everyone involved without a lot of explanation?

Measures used by competitors to evaluate and reward performance can be easily obtained from public filings, such as the annual report or proxy statement, and can provide valuable insight into those metrics that are most important for the industry. The measures cited by analysts in well-researched company or industry reports can be similarly informative. Not only are these metrics a good indicator of what others consider useful, but there is a good chance they will be used by your shareholders and prospective investors for performance and remuneration comparisons with other companies. This means they warrant periodic review from an investor relations perspective, even if not used explicitly to manage or reward performance. In addition, looking beyond direct competitors to those metrics used by similar businesses (based on capital intensity, customer focus, etc.) will challenge conventional wisdom and broaden choice.

While it may seem obvious, companies should not overlook the measures that have been used to assess and reward performance in the past. From a practical standpoint, these measures are already tracked regularly by the company, and employees have an established level of familiarity with them. Assuming they meet the other criteria outlined above (i.e., fit with the internal business context, shareholder alignment, and design applicability), metrics that have been used successfully in the past are generally preferable to other less familiar or more complicated measures.

Market research is a valuable first step, but companies need to go beyond the generic and deal with the specific. All companies are highly complex entities and no single measure fits all. What is your company's story and how do you tell it? In designing a comprehensive performance measurement system, the objective is to identify the business drivers that are *most* important in *your* unique company.

As we will see, this involves synthesizing a variety of qualitative and quantitative inputs. Statistical analysis of historical performance, current performance, and projections of future performance figures into this process. In addition, individual experience, intuition and judgment are the final arbiters of which drivers are selected. Good business sense cannot be neglected at any stage.

The Science of Metric Selection

How do you go beyond copying your competitors or using historical experience to develop a performance measurement system that meets the unique needs of your company? How do you develop your story? The number of factors to consider can be daunting—but fortunately there are tools to help identify the most appropriate metrics for your organization.

Business Model Analysis

One important consideration in selecting performance metrics is your company's business model (see Exhibit. 4.2). In the broadest sense, how does your company make money? How does it capture value from its customers? What are its sources of strategic control? Each company, even those within the same industry, has a unique approach to value creation. Large, diversified companies may use a combination of different approaches across the business.

A company's business model (or models) has important implications for measurement selection. Consider a company where the key asset is high brand recognition—for example, a popular series of films with a recurring action hero. Since the asset is unique and is owned and controlled exclusively by the company, it can leverage this key asset using a profit multiplier business model to extend the brand to other profit centers: action figure toys, a television cartoon character, theme park rides, books, cereal, a kids' clothing brand, and so on. Metrics for the profit multiplier model would probably include brand awareness, revenue growth, and profitability in each of these multiple lines of business.

Another example might be a business that introduces an innovative, attractive new product, such as a high-definition television. Although other companies can, and will, offer competing products, the television can, at first, be sold at a high price due to lack of immediate competition. As production continues, the costs drop; but growing

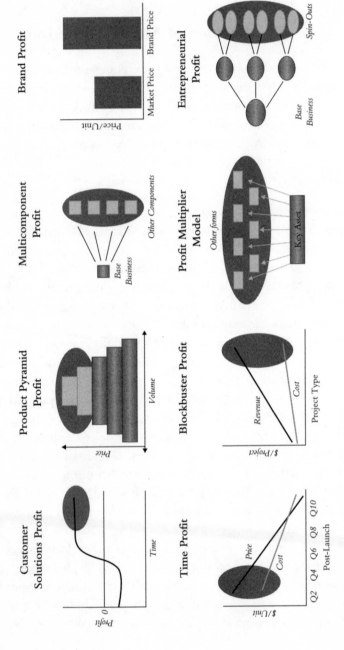

Exhibit 4.2   Some Common Business Models
SOURCE: Oliver Wyman.

competition and commoditization force the selling price down and, eventually, the product may become unprofitable. Performance metrics for companies with a time profit business model such as this often focus on market penetration or market share, as well as on extending the competitive life and profitability of the product. Since there is an understanding that the profitability of the product will erode over time, performance assessment at companies with this type of business model might also include strategic R&D goals that gauge progress toward bringing new products to market as quickly and efficiently as possible.

As a final example, take a company with a product pyramid profit model, such as a cell phone service provider. The company provides a variety of phone and service options at a range of different price points to maximize the number of subscribed users. Not all customers will purchase a high-tech phone or access high-margin features like ringtone downloads or GPS products right away, but the objective is to gradually build a base of dedicated customers who become more sophisticated users in time. Companies with this type of business model generally want to select a set of measures that encourage maximizing both the breadth and depth of customer relationships. For a cell phone company, this might mean measuring subscription growth in key markets in combination with tracking how well the company is marketing high-margin add-on services, using a metric such as average monthly bill per customer or average number of "products" sold per customer.

By understanding the models used to generate value at your company, you will have a more thorough understanding of the key levers of business success. This will enable you to design a measurement system that not only maximizes your competitive advantage, but also empowers your employees to better manage your business risks.

Value Driver Analysis

Once you understand, at a high level, how the company generates value, you can break down the process into more specific activities and behaviors by conducting a value chain analysis (see Exhibit 4.3). In this analysis, you start by identifying the primary levers of business success—revenues, operating expenses, invested capital, and so forth— which, together, lead to internal shareholder value creation. For each

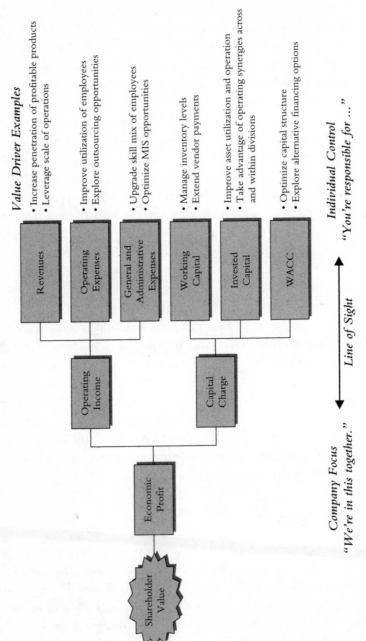

Exhibit 4.3   Sample Value Chain Analysis
SOURCE: Mercer.

of these factors, you then identify the specific activities that impact them. These activities, or value drivers, create line of sight between employee decisions and value creation.

In the example above, the company has identified several operating decisions that will reduce operating expenses, including using employees' skills more effectively and finding ways to outsource certain operations. Those value drivers that have the largest, manageable impact on value creation, and the metrics that capture them are what we described as *key success factors* (KSFs) in Chapter 2. In this case, some sort of productivity metric might be developed to track employee utilization, while a cost savings metric might be used to evaluate the success of outsourcing decisions.

A value driver analysis can be an extremely valuable tool. In complex companies, it will require input from a variety of different sources, and may even need to be broken down into a series of complementary analyses to accurately capture the contributions of different business units, functional groups or parts of the activity chain. In this sense, it can be useful for translating and cascading corporate level performance objectives (such as increase revenue by 10 percent year over year) into business unit, team, or individual goals (such as setting specific product revenue goals or establishing individual sales commission arrangements).

Regression Analysis

In addition to more qualitative inputs such as business model and value driver analyses, it is important to analyze and understand historical performance trends, including the relationship between financial performance and shareholder performance. There are many tools available for this purpose, beginning with a simple regression analysis to determine to what extent variations in stock price performance (dependent variable) can be explained by various measures of company performance (independent variable).

To conduct a regression analysis, a selected performance measure— EPS, for example—is plotted against a primary measure of external value creation, such as TSR, for the company and a group of comparable peers over a specified period of time (see Exhibit 4.4). The degree to which the two measures are correlated helps you gauge the usefulness

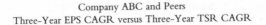

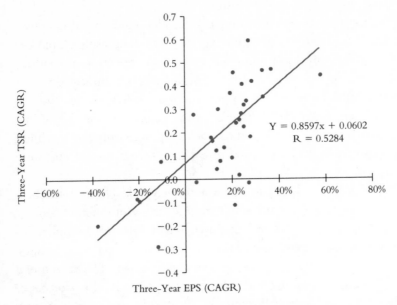

Company ABC and Peers
Three-Year EPS CAGR versus Three-Year TSR CAGR

Three-Year TSR (CAGR)

Y = 0.8597x + 0.0602
R = 0.5284

Three-Year EPS (CAGR)

Exhibit 4.4   Regression Analysis: Correlation of Performance Measure with Value Creation
SOURCE: Mercer.

and reliability of the performance measure as part of an incentive plan that will drive shareholder value creation.

Regression analysis can be used to test the suitability of metrics identified through other processes (such as value driver analysis), or can be used up-front to whittle down a wide range of potential measures into a smaller, more targeted group of metrics for further investigation.

Regression analysis can also be used near the end of the metric selection process to refine the definition of a selected metric or inform the design of incentive plans. For example, you could use regression analysis to compare alternative definitions of *return on invested capital* (ROIC), selecting the definition that provides the strongest correlation with external market value (see Exhibit 4.5). Since regression analysis can be performed over multiple time periods (for example, three or five years), it can also help identify the most appropriate time horizon for performance measurement, which could then be applied to the design of the long-term incentive program.

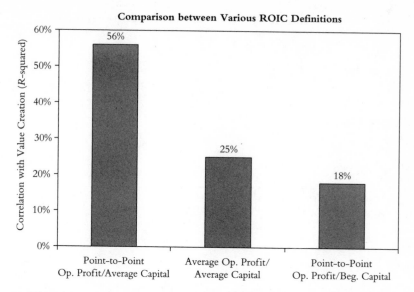

Exhibit 4.5 Summary of Regression Analysis Findings: Comparison of Various Definitions of ROIC
SOURCE: Mercer.

Time Series Analysis

Because regression analysis provides a point-in-time look at financial and market performance, it should be supplemented with a more in-depth look at financial and market performance trends over time. A time series analysis can often help validate the results of a regression analysis by providing a more illustrative look at the relationship between financial and market variables.

For example, by comparing your company's TSR movement against peers and the general market, you can confirm whether ups or downs in stock price can be explained by larger trends or are the result of specific actions taken by your company. When combined with financial performance trends, observable patterns often emerge. In Exhibit 4.6, total shareholder return is shown against EPS growth for a natural resources company. While the two measures seem to track each other to some extent, EPS appears to be much more volatile than TSR over time, which likely reflects the impact of commodity prices on the company's bottom line.

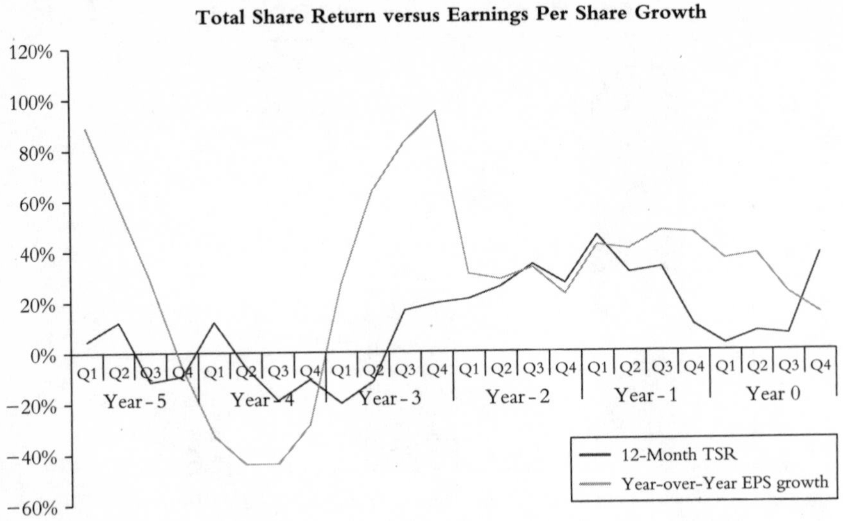

Total Share Return versus Earnings Per Share Growth

Exhibit 4.6   Time Series Analysis Showing EPS Growth versus TSR for
Natural Resources Company
SOURCE: Mercer.

Performance Sensitivity Analysis®

Another way to examine the relationship between company and market performance is to conduct a *performance sensitivity analysis*® (PSA). In
this analysis, which is proprietary to Mercer, a company's TSR volatility is compared to both industry peers and the general market over a
ten-year period. The extent to which the company's stock price moves
in concert with the industry or general market has important implications for what metrics would be most useful in managing and rewarding
performance.

Exhibit 4.7 presents the results of a PSA. Each company's market
behavior has been segmented into three categories: volatility caused by
the general market, volatility explained by industry fluctuations, and
volatility that can be attributed to company-specific factors. In this example, Company ABC's *total* stock price volatility is similar to the industry
median, but only 20 percent of this volatility is due to the company's
own activities, compared to a median firm-specific volatility of 45 percent. This suggests that fluctuations in Company ABC's stock price are
largely related to factors outside of management's control.

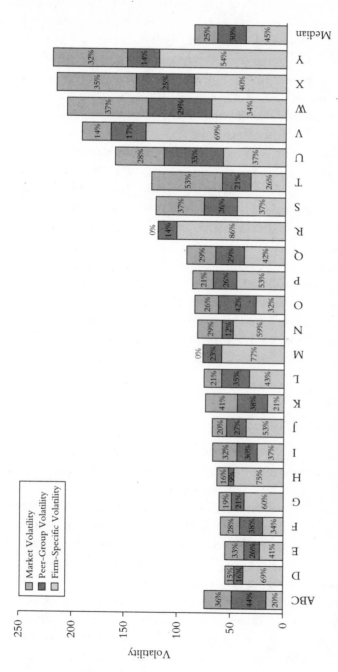

Exhibit 4.7 Performance Sensitivity Analysis® of Stock Price Volatility

SOURCE: Mercer.

NOTE: Due to rounding, the sum of the three components may not equal 100 percent.

The results of a PSA can inform your ultimate choice of metrics by giving you a sense of whether you need to look internally or externally when analyzing performance and calibrating executive pay. If, like Company ABC, your stock price is highly influenced by general market and industry trends, a measurement system that focuses on stock price or TSR goals may not provide sufficient line of sight to executive performance. Financial, operational, or strategic goals that executives would have more direct control over would likely be more effective at motivating and rewarding behavior.

In addition, PSA results have implications for peer group selection, goal setting, and long-term incentive plan design. PSA can be used to select credible peers by identifying companies with similar market risk profiles. PSA results can also inform whether goals should be set on an absolute or relative basis: companies whose stock price is highly sensitive to industry trends can help isolate firm-specific performance by measuring market results against peers. Along the same line, companies with significant firm-based volatility can rely more heavily on share price-oriented vehicles (e.g., options, restricted shares) when delivering long-term incentives, whereas companies with primarily market- and industry-related risk would be better off using performance shares or cash. We discuss each of these concepts in greater detail later in the book (see Chapters 6, 7, and 8).

Business Segment-Level Analysis

In large or diverse companies, it is important to understand the contributions of various parts of the business to value creation. For example, a large, mature unit of the company might play a critical role in generating cash to fund capital investments, while a smaller, emerging business is responsible for stimulating overall growth and driving shareholder expectations for future performance. Both are important functions that contribute to the overall success of the organization, but the financial results of each unit would be drastically different and the metrics and targets used to judge performance may need to be different as well.

One way to get an understanding of how the business units create value is to conduct an economic profitability analysis across the business. Other measures can be used for this analysis, but the key is to take a consistent view of performance across the various segments. In

Exhibit 4.8, the economic profit spread (i.e., the difference between the cost of capital and the return on invested capital) is shown for each business unit on the Y-axis, with the amount of capital invested in the unit represented on the X-axis. Breaking down the overall profitability versus investment in this way allows you to quickly see where value is being created and destroyed; the area of each bar represents the amount of positive or negative economic profit being generated by each unit.

In this example, two-thirds of this portfolio is performing under the cost of capital, which is resulting in a negative total corporate economic spread. In other words, the company as a whole is currently destroying value, rather than creating it. While this picture may very well inspire the company to reevaluate its strategic business priorities, it also has immediate consequences for the measurement system.

The units that are not currently covering the cost of capital (units A, C, and E) should be incentivized to improve their profitability as quickly as possible so that they can begin to cover the cost of the investments that have already been made in the business. This calls for a heavy emphasis on profitability or return-based metrics. On the other

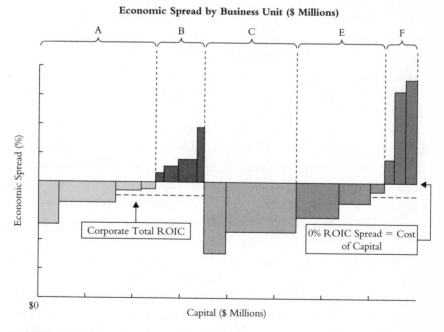

Exhibit 4.8 Contribution to Value Creation by Different Business Units
SOURCE: Mercer.

hand, the units that are already generating strong returns (units B and F) should be encouraged to actively grow the business so that the value creation model can be leveraged over a larger capital base. This suggests a focus on growth-related measures coupled, perhaps, with strategic goals that spell out the investments necessary to propel that growth.

Expectations Analysis

The performance measurement cycle outlined in Chapter 3 (see Exhibit 3.1) keeps returning to the phase where you diagnose outcomes and reevaluate your most important business drivers. Over time, your selection of performance metrics will change as your company grows, adjusts, and adapts to developments in the marketplace. Some of the changes you will encounter can be controlled, because they will depend on your own business planning and your ability to read trends and project them into the future. Others are beyond your control but can be prepared for and reacted to in a prudent and timely manner.

Internal processes and expectations are the most predictable influences on potential changes to the performance measurement system. During the strategic planning and budgeting processes, thought should be given to whether the existing measurement system continues to be relevant to the evolving goals of the organization. This is especially true in the case of strategic planning, as this is the time when companies vet the proper response (or formally acknowledge shifts that have taken place organically) to changes in the business environment.

During the planning process, it can also be helpful to review shareholder expectations for performance. While shareholder expectations may be gauged to some extent through informal polling (analysts reports), it is much more reliable to analyze the expectations that are embedded directly in a company's share price. Share price reflects the consensus opinion about how the company is performing today and how it is expected to perform going forward.

While shareholder expectations have obvious implications for goal setting (which we discuss in Chapter 7), they can also give you an idea how important growth is to the company's value. Exhibit 4.9 shows a situation in which a company's current-year operations ($650 million) accounted for slightly more than half the current external

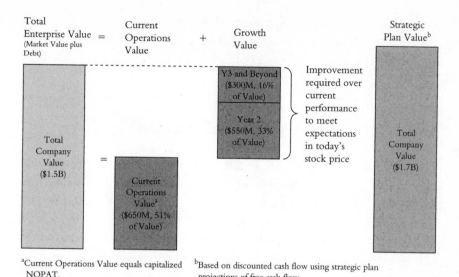

^aCurrent Operations Value equals capitalized NOPAT.   ^bBased on discounted cash flow using strategic plan projections of free cash flow.

Exhibit 4.9   Total Company Value Reflecting Shareholder Expectations of Growth
SOURCE: Mercer.

value of the company (far left); the rest was attributable to budgeted growth expected from sales of new products in the next year ($550 million) and beyond ($300 million). This meant that investors considered the company worth $850 million more than just the value of current operations and were expecting substantial growth in the near term. Although the strategic plan projected an additional $200 million growth beyond market valuation, there was no current recognition for it in the company's market value. It appeared that investors were not yet aware of the plan or discounted the company's capability to deliver this value. For this reason, the company would need to focus more heavily on growth measures than on profitability measures in order to meet and exceed shareholders' expectations.

The research methods and analyses presented above represent the *science* behind performance metric selection. Together, they provide hard facts and data that form the basis for selecting the metrics that will be the most effective in managing your business. Yet, as anyone who has spent time on a board or management team knows, things are not always as they seem. A metric that seems great on paper may not always work once it is put into play in a real organization. In some cases, it may just not fit well with the dynamics of the company (e.g., management model, decision-making process, availability of information); in others, it is not practical enough in its application. This is where good judgment and experience comes in.

The Art of Metric Selection

The *art* of metric selection involves using experience and good sense to interpret and apply the myriad of information available so that you may isolate those few performance metrics that will be most effective in managing your business. As outlined in Exhibit 4.1, the goal is to pick metrics that are well aligned with shareholder value creation, provide excellent fit with the organization, and are reasonable to apply in managing the business and rewarding performance. In the following section, we walk through some of the finer points in weighing various metric alternatives.

Simplicity versus Complexity

As discussed in earlier chapters, there is an inherent trade-off between accuracy and simplicity in your choice of metrics. The more complex (and, therefore, more accurate) the measure, the more reliable it will be in gauging just how well your company is performing. On the other hand, the simpler (and thus less accurate) the measure, the easier it is to understand, which may make it more effective both as a tool for motivating executive performance and as a guide for decision making at any level of the organization. It is a bit like the choice between taking the bus or driving a luxury car. The bus is cheaper and easier to use, but tends to be less reliable; whereas the luxury car is more expensive and more difficult to maintain, but will be more consistent and dependable in getting you from point A to point B.

The right balance between accuracy and complexity for any company depends on many things, including the existing corporate culture, the amount of time and resources available to invest in education and communication, and how broadly and deeply the performance measurement system will be applied. If your executives are financially literate and already have a strong sense of how your company creates value, it will be easier to implement a more complex measurement system that can assure more accurate results. However, if your management team does not have a strong understanding of financial concepts, it may be preferable to select simpler measures or migrate toward more complex measures over time in conjunction with an ongoing management education program.

Short Term versus Long Term

Shareholder pressure to produce impressive quarterly results—especially in terms of total shareholder return and earnings—often collides with shareholders' long-term interests for a company that is durable, stable, and capable of growing into an even more valuable investment over many years. For example, it is wise to remember that TSR, although it is simple and widely understood, is not a particularly good metric to use in a short-term incentive plan because stock price is influenced by external forces and intangible factors that may or may not reflect the realities of the company's actual business performance at any given time. An executive's outstanding performance should not be solely driven by hiccups in the economy, whether general or confined to an industry or a sector. Nor should the executive be rewarded inappropriately by one-time market-based events that may occur in the near or distant future.

In designing a performance measurement system, metrics should be chosen to provide balance in focus between short-term financial, operational, and strategic results and long-term shareholder value creation. This can be accomplished by choosing complementary metrics that represent all four dimensions in Mercer's performance measurement framework (see Chapter 3; Exhibit 3.7): growth, profitability, returns, and shareholder experience.

Global Businesses

For multinational companies, the situation is further complicated by differences in regional economies, exchange rates, local laws and regulations, languages, cultures, and myriad other factors. Performance measurement on a global scale may also involve multiple business models, organizational systems, and financial structures within a single organization that must be tied together with a common business language. The more complex the company, the more critical the performance measurement system; without a shared understanding of business priorities, different geographies can easily end up working at cross purposes.

Here is a case in point—a cautionary example of how *not* to design a global performance measurement system. A large professional services firm with offices around the globe saw that it needed to transform itself from a collection of locally oriented operations to a true worldwide organization. Communication and cooperation between its regional operations was hobbled by each region's focus on maximizing business locally and there was little incentive for executives to share their considerable expertise with other offices. To fully realize its global potential, the company would have to break down these operational silos and share their human and financial resources.

One problem was that the company was organized primarily around geographic units, using different business models in different parts of the world. Meanwhile, clients were increasingly demanding seamless solutions, regardless of geography. There was a company-wide problem as well: a decline in demand for key service areas was putting pressure on growth and margins. The business needed a new growth model that would break down its geographic compartmentalization and transform it into a truly global organization.

Toward that objective, the company developed a common talent management and rewards framework around the globe. Every region had the same career levels and the same reward opportunity based on individual performance ratings. However, it failed to establish common performance measures across geographies, and continued to fund incentive pools based on geographic profitability. The result? Even though the top leaders believed they had established a consistent approach, actual performance measurement and executive remuneration continued to vary widely from region to region. Local managers continued to have authority over the assignment of local teams and give top priority to the needs of their own markets. Cooperation with others outside the region remained difficult—and rare.

In this circumstance, the measurement system failed to support the organizational design changes that were needed to capitalize on new market opportunities that demanded seamless global solutions. If an organization creates value for shareholders through significant cross-border collaboration like the professional services company above, then its performance metrics should be largely consistent across regions. A centralized or uniform approach will also benefit companies that use the same business model throughout the entire network of operations, such as online marketplaces and networking sites that provide consistent applications around the world in order to develop a critical mass of users.

A consistent performance measurement system, however, is not a mandate for global firms. To determine if a global, regional, or local approach is better suited to your company, you must understand how to create shareholder value across the global business. If an organization has different business models and creates value differently through a range of disparate business units, then a variable system that responds to these inconsistencies is likely to be more effective in measuring and evaluating performance results. For example, a bricks-and-mortar retailer expanding operations outside the United States in order to sustain growth may discover it needs different business models in different geographies to be profitable in those areas. In this situation, market-specific performance measures designed to support the geographically based business models will more effective than a uniform global performance measurement system.

A Balancing Act

There are many ways to assemble a performance measurement system from the rich treasury of metrics that are available. No one way is absolutely correct or absolutely incorrect, but some are more defensible than others. We discuss tactics for developing a framework for applying performance metrics in the next chapter. Generally, however, a system that works well for both management and reward purposes should be based on:

- More than one metric
- The same metrics that indicate whether the organization's goals are being met

- Metrics that, if incentives are tied to relative performance, allow direct and meaningful comparisons with peers
- Metrics that support the interests of shareholders

Selecting the right metrics is an exercise in balance and finesse as much as it is hard analytical reasoning. One of the common errors in selecting performance metrics is the tendency to look at just one of the analytical tools described above and use it to justify a measure that has been used in the past or because members of the board or management are already comfortable with it. This is a shortcut through an inherently complex process, and it often produces misleading, inadequate, or nondefensible results.

A better mind-set is to go into the process without preconceptions about what you will discover. More often than not, when you bring together five or six independent analyses, consistent themes become apparent and a story begins to emerge. Suddenly, you see in front of you a performance measurement system that yields a logical business case with defensible results. In the end, the selection of defensible performance metrics will be a matter of judgment, informed by facts, research, experience, and intuition.

Chapter 5

Making It Count

*The Case for the Unbalanced Scorecard
to Drive Behavior*

S electing the right metrics is a vital step in ensuring a meaningful link between executive pay and performance. But companies also need to develop a workable framework under which the metrics can be applied to manage and reward business results. This framework is the key to moving from *measurement* to *management*. It provides a basis for the final step in the performance management continuum: initiating the behavioral change processes that truly drive executive performance.

This is by no means an easy exercise. There have been thousands of books written on the subject, and nearly as many methodologies espoused by everyone from academics to consultants to government officials. While there is a glut of brand-name approaches available to companies (think Economic Value Added, management by objective or Total Quality Management, for starters), none of these is a worthy substitute for a performance measurement framework that has been tailored to the unique strategic context of the business. A better bet than choosing an off-the-shelf solution is to follow a set of guiding principles culled from the very best ideas available to develop a customized approach that is poised to achieve real results within your distinct business environment.

While customization is paramount, this does not mean that you need to start from scratch. An excellent place to begin translating your selected metrics into a workable performance measurement framework is to adopt a scorecard approach. Unlike the Balanced Scorecard developed by Robert S. Kaplan and David P. Norton, scorecards need not be formulaic, but rather can be viewed as a highly flexible tool that can be adapted to nearly any situation. As we will build a case for later in the chapter, the scorecard of the future has no predefined performance dimensions, no set number of quadrants and no steadfast rules stating that there must be balanced emphasis on the various performance factors identified. In fact, Mercer strongly believes that in most cases an *unbalanced* scorecard—one that purposefully emphasizes the most critical priorities of the business—will achieve much more robust results than a diffuse system that sends weak or conflicting signals to executives.

Since much thinking has already been done on how to motivate and reward business results, this chapter begins by reviewing three notable pay-for-performance frameworks developed in recent history. Based on real-life company experiences with these and other measurement approaches, we identify a set of best practices that companies should follow in developing a performance measurement approach that fits with the strategic context of the business. We also discuss the evolution of the performance scorecard concept, building a case for unbalanced scorecards as a highly customizable tool that can be used to capture the multiple dimensions of performance at any organization.

Try, Try Again

Since the emergence of large corporations, people have been trying to figure out how to best measure and reward executive performance. Unfortunately, if it were that easy, someone would have figured it out decades ago and we would not see the debate continued in the board-room and on the front page of the business section year after year. Still, much can be gained by reviewing some of the key ideas that have been developed to date.

Earnings per Share

Many corporations use *earnings per share* (EPS) as the primary measure of business performance. EPS is one of the most common metrics used in executive annual incentive plans around the globe and in some industries, such as manufacturing, profit-sharing plans (which are typically pegged to EPS projections) are used to reward employees at all levels of the organization. EPS is also a popular measure in long-term incentive plans; in the United Kingdom, multiyear EPS targets are commonly used (alone or in combination with TSR goals) as the criteria for equity vesting.

The allure of EPS-based incentive plans is easy to understand. EPS is widely recognized and understood by the investment community, with the market often reacting visibly to quarterly EPS announcements. It is also a relatively simple and straightforward measure that provides clear line of sight to individual behaviors. While many executives struggle to understand how to impact more complex measures, such as returns, they generally know that they can influence EPS by increasing sales or cutting costs. Given this level of familiarity, both internally and externally, it is no wonder so many companies turn to EPS as a way to respond to shareholder concerns that executive remuneration be more closely tied to performance results.

However, there are several limitations to EPS as a unitary measure of performance. Too much emphasis on EPS is commonly criticized for encouraging management to make short-sighted decisions that maximize profits at the expense of building long-term shareholder value. EPS can also be influenced by share buy-backs, changes in accounting policy (such as the way inventories are tracked), or by shifts in the capital structure of the business. From a more practical sense, EPS growth calculations can be distortive when the base figure is negative or small, making comparisons against peers difficult.

While EPS is a simple and widely understand concept that can be a useful performance indicator, rigid applications of this or any other single metric often fail to provide a truly meaningful perspective on value creation. Investors buy and sell shares for myriad reasons, value investing being but one (value investing being the idea that a company is undervalued and thus the price of the stock is low relative to its true value). A study conducted by Paul Myners in 2001, on behalf of the Chancellor of the Exchequer in the United Kingdom, found other reasons, including the need of a fund (mutual or hedge) to conform to an indexing requirements, the desire to manage to a particular risk profile or to achieve a short-term goal for fund performance. Clearly, a more comprehensive approach to measurement is needed to capture long-term value creation.

EVA®—Economic Value Added

The Economic Value Added (EVA[1]) approach developed by Stern Stewart & Co in the 1980s was hailed by many as the solution to the challenge of aligning executive remuneration with performance. In a series of literally weighty books, Stern Stewart & Co outlined the main concepts behind EVA and detailed how the concept of EVA could be used not only to measure performance, but also to drive management decision making and determine executive incentive awards over both the short and long term.

The EVA approach argues against focusing on external indicators of shareholder value, since stock price is reflective of many factors outside of the control of the executive team. Instead, EVA advocates that true economic value is created when the return on capital exceeds the cost of that capital. In other words, value is created by executives when economic profit is generated.

The EVA approach is a seductive one. As discussed in Chapter 3, economic profit is a strong predictor of external shareholder value over time, and measurement systems that focus on controllable business factors can be highly effective in influencing behavior. EVA also represents an integrated, systematic approach to value management that emphasizes the alignment of a wide range of processes, rather than focusing on only one aspect of the performance measurement system, such as incentive remuneration.

---

[1]EVA® is a registered trademark of Stern Stewart & Co.

Despite its apparent advantages, many companies that have implemented an EVA-based measurement system have met with mixed results. For starters, EVA is a complex metric, made even more sophisticated by the hundreds of adjustments that can be incorporated into its definition to address specific business issues. This makes it difficult to educate executives on how their individual actions impact EVA, let alone to cascade the metric down to lower levels of the organization. Given the number of adjustments that can be made, EVA is also subject to criticisms of manipulation.

Not surprising given its complexity and broad application, the EVA approach can be quite burdensome to administer, requiring a large group of dedicated employees to support it. At some point, the costs of such a large-scale system can start to outweigh the benefits.

Some companies have also found there to be an awkward disconnect between the measurement system and actual shareholder experience. For example, the EVA approach recommends that a portion of the incentives earned annually be banked and paid out over time to reduce the impact of business cyclicality on executive remuneration. The intent is to eliminate any incentive for short-sighted decision making and excessive risk taking and to retain talent during temporary performance downturns. While these are worthy goals, they present challenges from an optical sense. While shareholders applaud efforts to ensure rewards reflect sustainable performance results, particularly in light of government bailout of many financial institutions, this approach requires significant investment in stakeholder education and ongoing communication. Companies do not want to be seen as paying too generously in years where performance is below par, even though the payment was earned previously when performance was strong.

Balanced Scorecard

First introduced in the late 1980s, the Balance Scorecard was developed as a way to address some of the issues found wanting with EVA and other highly quantitative measurement methodologies. Norton and Kaplan wrote a number of articles describing and discussing the approach in the early 1990s, which culminated in their book *The Balanced Scorecard*.

The Balance Scorecard made a significant contribution to thinking on performance measurement issues by highlighting a fact that had been forgotten by many: Financial metrics are extremely important, but they are not the only important measures. Financial metrics measure the outcome of a wide range of strategic and operational activities. But other quantitative and qualitative metrics, such as those directly related to the customers, employees, and internal processes of the business, can provide a more complete picture of performance results.

Norton and Kaplan prescribed a scorecard with metrics identified in four quadrants: Financial, Customer, Internal Business Processes, and Learning and Growth. True to its name, the Balanced Scorecard approach advocates that companies place equal emphasis on all four of the quadrants.

One of the clear advantages of the Balanced Scorecard approach is its ability to create clarity around overall corporate performance criteria and then cascade the criteria downward through the process of identifying related performance goals at the unit, group, team, and ultimately, individual level. If applied correctly, the scorecard becomes a vehicle for translating the business strategy into measurable activities throughout the organization.

Yet, as with EVA, many companies have struggled putting the Balanced Scorecard into practice. Four quadrants with multiple goals in each quadrant result in a very elaborate system that may be limited in its ability to focus and drive behavior. A related concern is that an equal balance between quadrants and measures does not send a clear and actionable message to employees regarding the priorities of the business. Put another way, when everything is important, nothing is.

Some companies have also had difficulty applying a prototype-driven design to their organization. In particular, the four quadrants identified by Norton and Kaplan may not adequately reflect a company's unique business strategy and culture. The value drivers at a legal firm are significantly different from the factors that impact value creation at a health care company; trying to conform the relevant performance metrics of such dissimilar organizations to fit within a single framework can be a counterproductive exercise.

Another limitation of the Balanced Scorecard is that, due to its complexity, it may not be dynamic enough to change with the business over time. For example, a transportation company that is shifting its market offering from trucking services to customized logistical solutions may find it difficult to effect the behavior changes necessary to execute on this strategy by using the same scorecard quadrants it has relied on the past. While the specific metrics used in each quadrant could be revised, such adjustments may not be sufficient to delineate the shifting priorities of the business.

Finally, while the Balanced Scorecard has proven very useful as a framework for communications and tracking, it is often difficult to integrate with other corporate processes such as remuneration and planning. A telemarketing company may very well want to encourage its sales associates to develop their skills, identify potential improvements in existing sales pitches, and suggest product enhancements that meet customer needs, as prescribed by the Learning and Growth, Internal Business Processes, and Customer quadrants. However, given the dynamics of the business, the company will most likely want to reward these individuals largely (if not entirely) based on results in the Financial quadrant, making a *balanced* scorecard unsuitable for the purpose of determining incentive remuneration.

From Solutions to Guiding Principles

The shortcomings of the methodologies described thus far attest to the fact that there is no single approach to performance measurement that work for all companies. Performance measurement cannot be seen as a solution in and of itself—it is merely a tool to help manage the company.[2] Like other management initiatives, the performance measurement approach must be derived from the business strategy and tailored to fit with the organization given cultural considerations and the external business context.

Still, there are certain best practice principles that can be identified to assist companies in applying selected performance metrics to

---

[2]While the performance measurement framework should be thoughtful, it need not be so comprehensive that it addresses each and every situation that might arise and documents them with hundreds of pages. There are certain baseline issues that are assumed to be incorporated. For example, adherence to the company's core values, compliance with legal and statutory guidelines, and alignment with the company's ethical policies. In today's environment and to ensure companies are now explicitly communicating them to plan participants so the framework's alignment to them is more important than ever. Additionally, more compensation arrangements, particularly short- and long-term incentive plans, include clawback provisions to help assure adherence to compliance standards.

manage the business and reward executives. Through our work with thousands of companies, we have found that the most successful performance measurement frameworks have three common characteristics: they are motivational, meaningful, and fair.

Make It Motivational

A motivational performance measurement framework requires two key things: strong line of sight to individual executive behaviors and linkage to appropriate organizational level. If these things are lacking, the incentive program will fail to deliver on the desired results, no matter how great the rewards.

Line of Sight

To effectively motivate people, they must feel that their efforts will be accurately reflected during the performance assessment process. This means that executives must be able to meaningfully impact the metrics being evaluated. If the performance evaluation process measures factors beyond the control or influence of executives, it may fail to motivate them into action, or worse, it may inadvertently motivate the wrong behaviors as individuals overstep the boundaries defined by their roles in an effort to wield an impact.

This begins with the occasionally difficult task of distinguishing between correlation and causality. Just because two factors are related, does not mean that one causes the other. For many years, researchers argued that eating breakfast caused students to perform better. Yet, eating breakfast is correlated with numerous other factors that influence student achievement, such as absenteeism. After controlling for these other factors, it appears that eating breakfast only makes a difference in the achievement of undernourished children—not the general population.

Line of sight describes the extent to which executive behaviors are causally related to the selected metrics. The top sales executive, for example, has strong line of sight to revenue metrics since his strategic decisions directly impact the sales of the company's products or services. The top product design executive also has line of sight to revenue results since her actions impact customer demand, although the impact is less direct.

Line of sight comes down to two related concepts: control and influence. In the examples above, the actions of both the sales executive and the product design executive affect revenue generation, but the nature and degree of the impact differs. The sales executive has control over revenue generation, while the product development executive has influence over revenue generation. It may be sensible to tie both executives to revenue results to some degree, but the company must be aware of the distinction between control and influence in order to avoid unintended consequences.

To illustrate this potential pitfall, consider a complex metric like employee turnover. The drivers of turnover are numerous—remuneration, career opportunities, hiring practices, external economic conditions, and managerial relationships, to name just a few. While the director of remuneration may be able to *influence* turnover, employee turnover is not within his span of control. If his performance is evaluated based on turnover results, he may be encouraged to take actions that *are* within his control—such as raising remuneration levels across the business— in an attempt to move the measure. The result may or may not be lower turnover rates, but the unintended consequences are that the employment costs of the business have been increased, while other potential factors leading to turnover have been ignored.

If retention is a priority of the business, a better approach might be to introduce a shared goal that recognizes the interdependencies involved in working toward this objective. For example, the director of remuneration, business unit human resources representative, and business unit head might have shared accountability for improving retention in the business unit.

Generally, a company's most senior executives are considered to have strong line of sight to overall corporate results. While specific individuals may have more or less control over certain measures, the senior executives are collectively responsible for setting the strategic direction of the business and providing direction and oversight for executing on that strategy. If the strategy turns out to be ineffective or execution is poor, accountability for the lackluster results ultimately resides with that same group. On a related note, measuring senior executive performance largely based on corporate-wide metrics sends a strong message about the close collaboration and cooperation expected from the executive team.

Below the senior management level, the focus in measuring performance moves from strategy to tactics. Different roles have different purposes and the business strategy itself sets the criteria for performance evaluation. For example, if the senior management team of an airline determines that the company will hedge its fuel contracts in anticipation of rising fuel prices, the performance criteria for the top procurement executive becomes the successful execution of this strategy. If the strategy backfires and fuel prices decline in the coming years, the senior executives should be held responsible for the negative impact on profitability, but the procurement executive should not; his span of control was in negotiating favorable contracts, not in setting the business strategy. Of course, incentive payments at all levels of the organization may be influenced by the overall financial health of the company, but it is important that the messages sent regarding performance evaluation emphasize those factors that are most within the control of the contributor.

Organizational Linkage

Linkage is an idea that is related to, but not identical to the concept of line of sight. It describes the degree to which executives are rewarded based on corporate versus business unit versus team or individual performance results. While control and influence are important considerations in determining the appropriate organizational level on which to evaluate performance, proper linkage will also be a function of the business strategy and work culture.

In cases where significant synergies exist across the business and the overarching strategy for creating shareholder value (as defined by the senior management team) depends heavily on cross-collaboration and cooperation, companies should place greater emphasis on performance at higher levels of the organization. For example, a software company, whose products leverage similar technologies and serve overlapping customer bases, might focus on overall corporate results when evaluating the performance of business unit executives so as to encourage partnering across the business. On the other hand, a holding company with diverse business units that essentially function as separate entities would have less need for business unit leaders to interact and, therefore, might focus more on business unit results or individual accomplishments when measuring performance.

Measuring performance at higher levels of the organization may be pertinent in situations where the success of one business unit could have a negative impact on the results of another. Consider a copier company whose design engineers are working to improve the reliability of the company's products in support of the business strategy. Their ability to execute on this goal may depend on feedback obtained from field service technicians while, paradoxically, their success in making a more reliable copier could possibly cannibalize the revenue of the service unit by reducing the market demand for repair work. A carefully designed performance measurement framework must recognize potential performance trade-offs and measure results at a level that will support rather than thwart execution of the business strategy.

Similarly, a company whose culture emphasizes team-based work methods may choose to measure performance largely at the group or team level, rather than focusing on individual accomplishments. On the other hand, a company with a talent strategy that encourages independent thinking and entrepreneurialism may prefer to measure and reward individual contributions.

Most companies find value in measuring executive performance at a combination of organizational levels, so the issue is not really what level of the organization to measure performance at but rather how much weight to place on results when determining incentive awards. A helpful question to ask is, "Why does this job exist?" Members of the senior management team are often considered corporate assets that exist to build value of the corporation and, therefore, their performance is best measured based on the enhancement of this asset. In other words, the large majority of incentives for the CEO, CFO, and other senior executives should be linked to corporate-level results.

On the other hand, executives that head business units are largely concerned with maximizing business unit value and, therefore, should be compensated primarily based on business unit performance. But since business unit heads also play an important role in shaping the overall corporate strategy, their incentives should also be tied in part to corporate results. The specific balance between corporate and business unit weightings should reflect the job design, as well as the organizational and strategic factors outlined above.

While these best practice principles can be applied in most situations, it is important to note that more targeted incentive arrangements may be warranted for individuals with unique, nonmanagerial roles in the company. Technological innovators or corporate figureheads often play a crucial role in the success of the business and should be measured and rewarded in a way that reflects their special contributions. Exhibit 5.1 provides an example of how one company put this and other concepts related to linkage into action by crafting metric weightings based on executive title.

Linkage should be a consideration not only in determining performance measure weightings, but also in choosing incentive vehicles. For example, highly leveraged equity vehicles, such as indexed stock options or performance shares, may be suitable for executives with a strong line of sight to corporate performance, but inappropriate at lower levels of the organization where an employee's day-to-day activities are far removed from stock price fluctuations. A cash-based, short-term incentive plan focused on metrics more directly related to their contributions would likely be more effective at motivating individuals below the executive level.

Executive Level	ABC Co. Performance Evaluation Weighting		
	Corporate Metrics	Unit/Function Metrics	Individual/Team Metrics
CEO, CFO, COO	100%	—	—
Chief Innovator	—	—	100%
EVPs	60%	40%	—
SVPs	40%	60%	—
VPs	30%	50%	20%

Exhibit 5.1   Example of Organizational Linkage in Annual Incentive Plan
SOURCE: Mercer.

Make It Meaningful

In addition to being motivational, the performance measurement framework must be meaningful to the executive in order to influence behaviors. Executives must understand exactly what is being asked of them, and must trust that the goals and objectives identified are in the best interest of themselves and shareholders.

Clarity of Message

Managers must sort through hundreds of competing signals in making decisions each day, so the performance measurement system and incentive remuneration programs should strive to add clarity, not complexity, to the work experience. This requires conveying a clear message about performance expectations so as to avoid unintended consequences. It also requires focusing on the most critical dimensions of performance rather than overloading executives with a litany of disparate goals.

The best performance measurement frameworks skillfully translate the strategy for the business into activities that can be executed on the ground. An excellent example of sending a clear and coherent message regarding the priorities of the business can be found in retail industry, where a major grocery chain adopted merchandising as the center of its business strategy. Noticing that its competitors managed its business largely based on financial metrics like volume and margins, it pushed the emphasis on merchandising down throughout the organization by utilizing metrics that captured customer behaviors (like average transaction size) in measuring and rewarding performance. Everyone in the organization—from the chief financial officer to product buyers to stock clerks—was forced to ask themselves how the customer experience would be impacted by their decisions. The company reinforced this strategy by communicating performance results widely and frequently through actions such as posting sales results where all employees could view them.

Examples where the business strategy was not so clearly communicated through the performance measurement system are numerous. Take the international airline that decided to compete head to head with emerging no-frills competitors by rolling out a new brand focused on regional flight services. While the strategy itself reflected a reasonable response to the changing market, it failed miserably and the offshoot carrier was eventually grounded with major financial losses to the corporation. The problem lay in the execution of the strategy; the low-cost offshoot carrier was built using the exact same cost model as the parent airline, while ticket prices were set to compete in a very different market. If the airline had designed its performance measurement system around those factors that were most critical to the success of the venture—such as meeting stringent operating margins—those responsible for executing the strategy may have better understood the need to shift their approach from "business as usual" to something radically different.

Another place where companies can go wrong is in overloading executives with a long list of goals, each of which is tied to a small fraction of the incentive remuneration opportunity. While it is true that there are many factors that contribute to business success, too many metrics dilutes the message the company is striving to communicate about the business strategy. A collection of unrelated goals does nothing to delineate the priorities of the business and, in fact, can make it impossible to "see the forest for the trees."

Under the best-case scenario, executives will put in similar efforts across the metrics, achieving mediocre results on all. In the worst case, executives will pick and choose the goals they *want* to focus most closely on, which may or may not be the same goals that they *should* be focused on to maximize shareholder value. When a company discovers its performance goals are too numerous, or an external development or shift in business strategies renders the existing measurement system obsolete, they must go back to the drawing board. This generally means modifying the measurement system prior to the next performance cycle, but some cases may warrant immediate corrective action to salvage the motivational value of the plan or avoid unintended consequences that could negatively impact the business. In Chapter 9, we discuss ways to address this and other challenges that may arise during the performance measurement process.

To identify the KSFs—key success factors—that contribute disproportionally to success, companies must go back to the business strategy. For example, in the face of rising health care costs and tightening margins, hospitals began tracking the costs of everything from overnight stays to patient meals. Yet, in trying to manage costs by focusing on the smallest minutiae they had lost sight of the fact that the purpose of their organization was to save lives. By refocusing efforts on the fundamental mission of the business, they uncovered one of the biggest costs to the business: medical mistakes. Reducing preventable errors has not only improved care and saved lives, but has also cut costs by eliminating the need for repetitive or follow-up care and lowering medical malpractice insurance premiums. There have been many auxiliary benefits of initiatives designed to reduce medical mistakes as well, such as improving the flow of information between doctors, nurses, and administrators and improving the patient experience.

Flexibility

In order for the performance measurement system to remain meaningful over time it must be adaptable enough to change with the circumstances that surround it. Specifically, companies must have the ability to introduce new metrics or adjust metric weightings in light of shifting business priorities or changes to the organizational structure.

A flexible framework also enables the company to be *appropriately* opportunistic. A measurement system embedded in past successes is doomed for failure, because what makes you a winner today will not make you a winner tomorrow. Competitors will always borrow and improve upon your ideas, so executives must constantly strive for the next big thing that will maintain the company's competitive edge in the marketplace. A flexible performance measurement framework will enable the business to look to the future and measure those factors that will lead to value creation tomorrow, rather than focusing on those things that have created value in the past. As we discuss later in the chapter, incorporating a balance of short- and long-term financial measures further helps orient the measurement system toward the future by encouraging executives to take calculated risks, rather than blindly chasing after the *fad du jour* for a quick win.

Many organizations recognize the need to adjust the measurement system when they mature or reinvent themselves in new ways. For example, one aircraft manufacturer faced a drop in the demand for its products as the global market for air travel retracted as a result of the growing threat of terrorism and rises in fuel prices. Recognizing this trend, the company's emphasis in measuring performance shifted from growth to cost containment in an effort to maximize the value of remaining contracts and generate a sufficient amount of cash to reinvest in new areas of the business. In recent years, research advancements have led to the transformation of aircraft systems from hydraulic to electronic actuation. Among the many advantages of this redesign are a lighter aircraft (leading to a decrease in fuel consumption), lower maintenance costs, and an increase in the life of the engine. This has created renewed market demand, and the company will again need to revise its measurement system to maximize the full potential of this development.

Sound and Compelling Vision

Just as important as the message itself is how the message will be *perceived* by the different audiences that receive it. In order to drive changes in executive behavior, executives must believe that the business strategy, as captured by the performance measurement system, is sound, achievable, and aligned with their interests. This requires a high degree of self-confidence on the behalf of the leaders of the company, as well as a keen understanding of the external world in which the company operates.

One well-documented failure to provide a compelling vision for workers can be found in the history books. During World War II, Germany used slave labor to manufacture weapons. Since the workers knew it was not in their best interest for the Nazis to achieve military success, they purposely sabotaged the munitions they made so that they would malfunction and injure the user. These munitions malfunctions impeded the German's efforts to press farther into Europe and Russia, and eventually helped lead to the fall of the Nazi regime.

A more current example is the recent financial industry meltdown, which can largely be attributed to a lack of understanding and foresight on the part of the business leaders in the strategy they espoused. Financial instruments were evolving so quickly that only a handful of people fully understood the extent of the risks associated with mortgage-backed securities. As a result, managers were left to execute the business strategy without sufficient information to make informed decisions. The result has been huge write-offs across the industry, government buy-backs, and a ripple effect throughout the global economy.

Make It Fair

The final factor that makes or breaks a company's ability to apply performance metrics to drive behaviors and reward results is fairness. Frameworks that are multidimensional tend to be more accurate in capturing performance (and, accordingly, are perceived as being more just) than those that rely on only one or two inputs. This greatly improves the likelihood that the measurement framework will motivate performance.

Multidimensional

A performance measurement framework should strive to capture a variety of different aspects of performance (Exhibit 5.2). Multiple, complementary metrics provide a more complete picture of value creation than any single metric can, particularly when they reflect a range of financial, operational, and strategic outcomes. The most robust measurement systems use both qualitative and quantitative measures and

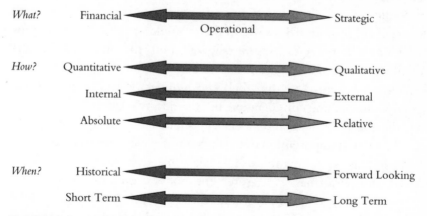

Exhibit 5.2   Multidimensional Performance Assessment
SOURCE: Mercer.

consider a mix of both historical and leading indicators of performance over the short and long term, while still maintaining a strong focus on the priorities of the business. In addition, a wide range of internal and external inputs should be considered in evaluating performance results, which may mean using a combination of absolute and relative measures.

Financial results are objective, easy to measure, and, because they can be calculated from publicly available accounting statements, tend to represent the shareholder perspective of performance. Yet, financial metrics lag other types of measures; they measure the culmination of a wide range of activities, rather than measuring the activities themselves. Relying exclusively on financial results to manage your business is like driving while looking through the rearview mirror.

Like financial measures, operational measures are quantifiable, but they provide enhanced line of sight to behavior. They aim to capture the subprocesses where improvement opportunities reside. Take a simple financial metric, like revenue. Revenue is the product of volume and price, and volume in turn is the product of a number of other factors. Operational metrics aim to measure those activities that impact financial results. In the case of volume, this could mean anything from the number of phone calls made by telemarketers at a direct sales company to the number of singles downloaded by customers of a music label.

Strategic measures, on the other hand, tend to be qualitative in nature, so evaluation is more subjective. Strategic measures are important indicators of where the business is headed and generally lead both financial and operational results. In the example of the music label provided above, a strategic measure that *leads* both the number of singles downloaded and annual sales revenues might be the value of new performance acts signed to the label. The number of acts (a quantifiable figure) would be one consideration, but the quality of those acts and how well those acts fit with the label's target audience (qualitative factors) would be just as important in evaluating performance on this metric.

Including a combination of financial, objective, and strategic measures in your performance measurement framework ensures a good mix of quantitative and qualitative and historical (lag) and forward-looking (lead) measures. However, as discussed earlier in the chapter, the objective is to choose a few well-balanced and complementary metrics, not to identify a gamut of unrelated goals that could divert attention from the most important performance issues. It is a fine line to walk, but one that can be achieved through in-depth analysis of historical performance results and careful deliberation on the part of the board and senior management regarding how to best support the go-forward business strategy.

As discussed in earlier chapters, a multidimensional approach to performance measurement also requires measuring performance over different periods of time. Near-term performance results are important but will only lead to value creation if they can be maintained and built upon over time. Measuring performance over both the short and long term ensures balance and fairness in the measurement system. If results don't get measured today, executives can expect that these results will be captured and rewarded in the future. At the same time, gaming short-term results to provide enhanced incentives today will end up hurting executives over the long term if the results are not sustainable.

Finally, the accuracy of the measurement system will be improved if performance assessments are informed by a wide variety of internal and external factors. Business results can only be assessed in relation to other things—be it the internal budget, general economic trends, or competitor performance. The more factors that are considered in setting performance targets, the more accurate (and fair) the performance assessment is likely to be. We discuss this point further in Chapter 7, which focuses on target setting and the advantages and disadvantages of absolute versus relative performance measures.

The Future of Scorecards

As we learned in reviewing the advantages and disadvantages of several popular frameworks for measuring and rewarding performance, narrow measurement approaches tend to fail because they do not fully capture performance or ignore the context in which the performance occurs. The Balanced Scorecard approach tried to rectify these limitations by incorporating multiple perspectives of performance, but some companies have found it to be too prescriptive to meet their organizational needs.

Yet, we should not throw out the baby out with the bath water. The scorecard concept is a valuable one, and it can be an excellent framework for applying the best-practice principles of motivation, meaningfulness, and fairness that have already been outlined in this chapter. The next generation of scorecards will continue to plan, communicate, and assess performance from a variety of perspectives. However, they will be simpler, less balanced, and tailored to meet the needs of the business (see Exhibit 5.3).

Traditional scorecards are complex and rigid, with value drivers selected to fit a prototype model. In contrast, the scorecard of the future will be simple and flexible, with value drivers derived from the company's profit model and current business strategy. Whereas traditional scorecards emphasize balance, the optimal scorecard will be focused on critical business priorities, enabling the company to send a clear and consistent message to executives regarding performance expectations. The most effective scorecards will also be sensitive to cultural issues, being adaptable enough to apply in highly disparate business units or across geographies.

Like metric selection, the scorecard design must reflect the strategic context of the business. The key is to focus on your unique profit model and business strategy, answering questions such as:

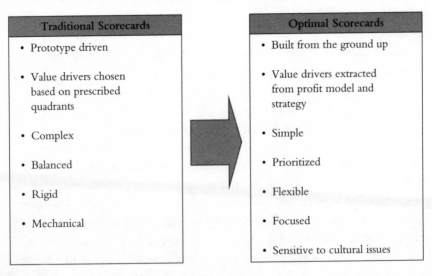

Traditional Scorecards	Optimal Scorecards
• Prototype driven	• Built from the ground up
• Value drivers chosen based on prescribed quadrants	• Value drivers extracted from profit model and strategy
• Complex	• Simple
• Balanced	• Prioritized
• Rigid	• Flexible
• Mechanical	• Focused
	• Sensitive to cultural issues

Exhibit 5.3   The Evolution of Performance Scorecards
Source: Mercer.

- What are the current business challenges?
- Which market segments are being focused on?
- What is the value proposition to our customers?
- How do we create and deliver value to our shareholders?
- What are our sources of competitive differentiation?
- What is the value of our brand?
- Are we seen as the "esteemed" provider?
- Are the products and services relevant today and tomorrow?
- Will the things that made us successful help fuel future success?

The answers to these and related questions will inform the design of the scorecard and enable you to identify those measures—the KSFs—that will have the highest impact on your business strategy given the current business context. The business strategy will also help you to determine the appropriate mix of financial, operational, and strategic measures, as well as the right linkage with enterprise-wide versus business unit versus team or individual measures.

To better understand how an unbalanced scorecard framework can be applied to reflect the strategic business context at your company, consider how one hospitality company followed the best-practice principles identified in this chapter to design and implement a common scorecard framework across its diverse organization.

The company owned a portfolio of related hospitality businesses, with each business unit confronting very different market conditions. Some units were experiencing high growth in an expanding market, while others faced more limited growth prospects and were shifting focus toward profit maximization. To make things more complicated, some units were operating in consolidating markets and undertaking merger and acquisition activities, so both the external environment and the internal structure of the organization were in a constant state of flux.

One of the key priorities of the business strategy was to focus on cross-marketing to leverage their brands, while still recognizing the realities of each market. The existing performance measurement framework was limited to a single set of financial metrics and weights for all businesses, combined with individual objectives for each executive.

The implications of this strategic context for the performance measurement system included the following:

- A common measurement framework is appropriate to emphasize cross business cooperation and the goal of realizing synergies.
- But, greater flexibility is required to tailor the measures and weights to the priorities of each business.
- In addition, selected strategic indicators are needed to capture the drivers of business success and emphasize common corporate goals.

The solution was a common scorecard framework that contained the flexibility to tailor measures and priorities to the needs of each business (see Exhibit 5.4). Rather than using set measures across all of the businesses, the new performance framework allowed for the customization of growth measures to reflect the strategic priorities of each business unit. In addition, while the performance of each unit would continue to be measured in part by Economic Value Added, the weight on the EVA metric relative to the selected growth metric(s) would vary depending on the unit's stage of maturity. Finally, individual performance objectives were replaced with strategic objectives that would be measured at either the corporate or business unit level (or both), depending on the desired linkage for each executive.

While similar in framework, the actual scorecards developed for each business unit emphasized their unique priorities. For example, in Exhibit 5.5, the hotel unit operated under a franchise model that led to high returns, but low growth relative to peers. As a result of market

Existing Performance Measurement Framework		Revised Scorecard Framework	
		Growth	**Returns**
BU operating profit	50%	• Measures tailored to each business unit	• EVA for all businesses
BU EVA	20%	• Weights between 20% and 50% depending on priorities	• Weights between 20% and 50% depending on priorities
Individual performance (performance objectives)	30%	**Strategic Objectives**	
		• 30% of scorecard for all businesses	
		• Two to three measures of common corporate priorities or selected business unit specific measures	

Exhibit 5.4   Hospitality Co. Scorecard Framework
SOURCE: Mercer.

Hotels		
Growth	**Returns**	
Revenues 20%	EVA 20%	
Profits 30%		
Strategic Objectives		
Corporate cost reduction		10%
Property growth goals		10%
Team specific goals		10%

Restaurants		
Growth	**Returns**	
Profits 40%	EVA 30%	
Strategic Objectives		
Corporate cost reduction		10%
Margin improvements		10%
Customer satisfaction		10%

Exhibit 5.5   Hospitality Co. Business Unit Scorecards
SOURCE: Mercer.

consolidation, the brand's market position was eroding, further limiting franchise opportunities. Recognizing these issues, a key strategic priority for the business was to grow revenues through owned properties. Given this context, the scorecard placed a significant emphasis on revenue and profit growth and included a strategic objective aimed at fueling property growth.

The restaurant business unit faced an entirely different set of challenges. Its mature brands were reaching the point of market saturation, which was severely hindering revenue improvement opportunities. Meanwhile, recent performance declines across the unit indicated a need to focus on reviving the company's current store base and improving profitability levels. The restaurant's scorecard included heavy emphasis on profit growth (40 percent weight), combined with a meaningful focus on returns, as measured by EVA. To further stress the importance of improving profitability, margin improvement was identified as a strategic goal for the business unit. And, since the company viewed its existing store base as critical to profit generation, it added another strategic goal focused on customer satisfaction.

To provide alignment with a key corporate objective of improving the cost structure across the business, executives in both the hotel and restaurant businesses were held to specific cost reduction goals.

The scorecard framework developed by Hospitality Co. successfully provides a common approach to performance measurement, while enabling the customization of the scorecard to specific business unit circumstances. In addition, it is flexible enough to change as the business evolves;

relevant strategic objectives are identified annually, while the weighting of selected growth and return metrics will be reviewed periodically to ensure they continue to reflect the priorities of each business.

Custom Solutions

There is no single perfect performance measurement solution because there are no two businesses that are alike. The best performance measurement system for your company will be unique, because it will be shaped by the strategic context of your business.

However, there are some universal principles that can be applied in developing a customized solution. The most effective performance measurement systems not only use the right metrics, but are motivational, meaningful, and fair. This requires strong line of sight to executive performance and careful consideration of the appropriate organizational level (or combination of organizational levels) to link performance evaluations.

The most effective performance measurement frameworks will also convey a clear and consistent message about the most critical priorities of the business and will demonstrate a robust understanding of the business and the world in which it operates. Because the business and the external context that influences it are in constant flux, the performance measurement system also requires sufficient flexibility to adapt with the business over time.

Finally, an effective performance measurement framework includes multiple viewpoints on performance. This framework balances the emphasis on historical and forward-looking results, incorporates both internal and external definitions of success, and includes a mix of financial, operational, and strategic measures.

A scorecard framework can help companies realize all of these objectives. The new and improved scorecard provides a multidimensional perspective of performance, but it is also simple and focused. It sets clear priorities linked to a company's current strategic situation and will not necessarily be evenly balanced. Most importantly, it will be embedded to a company's unique strategy for creating shareholder value.

Of course, to achieve maximum impact on executive behaviors, the scorecard—like any performance measurement framework—must be thoughtfully tied to reward programs. Among other things, this requires identifying appropriate peers for performance comparisons, setting reasonable targets, appropriately calibrating pay and performance outcomes, and dealing with unexpected measurement problems as they arise. The remaining chapters of this book focus on these challenges, which are the key to successfully applying your selected metrics and ensuing scorecard framework to drive business results.

Chapter 6

There's Nobody Quite Like Us

The Ins and Outs of Meaningful Peer Comparison

Decisions about compensating executives are the product of many factors, both internal and external to the company. Among external factors, companies have traditionally used peer groups to gauge the competitive talent market and evaluate company performance. A peer group—a set of organizations that share important characteristics—is considered a valuable reference because it consists of companies that operate in the same environment and are subject to the same human capital, economic, and capital market influences. As such, peer group practices provide a critical foundation for making decisions regarding both remuneration opportunity and program design.

In recent years, however, the peer group standard has come under greater scrutiny. Some feel that the "cherry-picking" of high-performing and high-paying peer companies has brought about an inflation of executive salaries. Sensitivity to peer group selection has increased for publicly traded companies as a result of more demanding disclosure rules requiring greater transparency of the amount and types of remuneration paid to top executive officers. Companies need to be able to articulate how peers are selected and how the peer group relates to decisions the company makes in compensating its top executives.

For companies that are not publicly traded, peer group selection is critical to ensure that the fact-base for decision making is reasonable and will result in appropriate decisions. Given these expectations, companies must employ a sound and defensible strategy for selecting and maintaining their executive remuneration peer groups.

In this chapter we discuss the art and science of peer group selection. We pose and answer a number of basic questions:

- What is the purpose of peer groups?
- How are they selected?
- What factors are considered in comparing other companies with your own?
- How many companies do you need, and what kinds, in a peer group?
- What circumstances warrant the use of more than one peer group?
- How do you use them to decide what to pay your own top executives?
- What other uses are there for peer groups?

These questions and others are important to making and defending decisions on the amounts and kinds of rewards your executives receive in return for services and the performance achieved.

Why Peer Groups?

At its core, the reason for identifying a peer group is to give your company a standard for comparison with other companies, particularly those you compete with for leadership talent. Peer group members are selected for their similarity in specific, measurable ways—such as size, complexity, industry, or risk profile—and thus serve as a basis for comparing your company's executive pay programs and pay levels with those in the peer group. Ideally, peer group selection should be based on objective criteria and should be conducted *before* examining any pay practices. This reduces the likelihood (and perception) that peer companies might be cherry-picked to yield predetermined conclusions about executive remuneration.

Once peer groups are chosen, they can be used for three different comparisons between your company and its peers.

1. *Pay magnitude.* What salary, benefits, and incentive award levels are competitive? Companies measuring pay magnitude look at competitive practices related to overall pay delivery, including base salaries, annual and long-term incentive targets and payouts, equity usage and executive benefit and perquisite programs. With more transparency required of them, companies are providing more detail in their proxy statements (or equivalent disclosure) on how key executives are paid, making it easier than ever to analyze the amount of remuneration delivered to executives annually and over the long term.

2. *Pay practices and program design.* How do other companies structure their remuneration programs? An assessment of the design attributes of other organizations' remuneration programs can provide perspective on pay strategy and linkages between pay and performance. Examples of pay practices that might be gleaned from this type of research include pay mix, performance metrics used in determining plan payouts, calibration of target, threshold and maximum payout opportunities against performance levels, approach to long-term incentive delivery, and change in control practices.

3. *Performance comparison.* Is pay aligned with performance? Peer group analysis can help determine if the amount a company pays executives is appropriately aligned with results. When comparing performance relative to peers, companies can not only assess if pay is directionally aligned with performance, but also incorporate this information into the goal-setting process for annual and long-term incentives, or use relative performance measurement against peers directly in incentive plan award calculations.

Regardless of the purpose, peer group research is just one input into the remuneration decision-making process. Careful judgment must be applied in analyzing and interpreting peer group data to ensure that remuneration decisions appropriately reflect your organization's unique business and executive talent needs. It is also important to remember that publicly disclosed remuneration information is only available for a handful of executive positions. To ensure a consistent approach for assessing pay practices across the entire executive group, you will want to supplement peer group research with data from other sources, such as published remuneration surveys.

Screening for Peers

Identifying a peer group is a process of applying a carefully chosen set of criteria to select, from a large number of candidates, a group of companies that are comparable to your own in certain important ways. Your peers are most likely to be businesses that are in your industry, serve many of the same customers, produce or sell similar products, are close to your company in size and complexity, and seek investment from the same sources.

Peers can also be thought of as companies whose executives are paid to manage risks similar to those faced by your own company—including financial, operational, capital, and labor risk. Remuneration programs and practices reflect these aspects of enterprise risk, which vary significantly among companies based on factors like industry and stage of business maturity. For example, industries such as entertainment or financial services typically experience more volatile performance (and risk) than industries like utilities. Reflecting these characteristics, pay magnitude and incentive use in the entertainment and financial services industries is much more significant than in utilities. Selecting peers that share common profiles helps support fact-based remuneration decisions that appropriately reward the successful management of risk and the achievement of business goals.

Peer group selection can be visualized as a process of sifting or screening for different attributes (Exhibit 6.1). For example, the first step is to screen for companies you compete with in several different types of markets; then narrow down the field by screening out

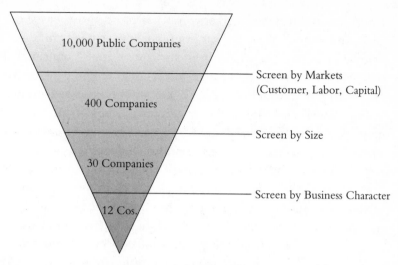

Exhibit 6.1   Screening for Peer Group (Example)
SOURCE: Mercer.

companies significantly larger or smaller than yours; finally, apply other carefully chosen criteria to focus on companies that are like yours in key ways, such as sharing the same business model or having a similar organizational structure. During each of these screens, judgment about fit should be applied so the process is not purely mechanical.

Screen by Markets

Your company, like all companies, competes in several different types of markets. The most obvious of these is the customer market, for which your company provides goods or services. Other competitive markets include labor, in which the competition is for talent, and capital, where companies vie for investment funding. These three markets, which overlap and are not mutually exclusive, represent the most significant criteria for peer group selection.

- *Customer markets.* Peer group candidates in this category are organizations that compete directly with you for customers and revenue. They may share your industry classification code and be the primary competitors in your product or service area, or they may offer similar products or services but not compete directly.

- *Labor markets.* The labor market consists of competitors for executive talent and may be organizations from which executives are recruited or to which executives have been or may be lost. Companies that compete with one another for customers tend to compete for executive talent as well, although this is not always the case. Particularly among larger companies, the competitive labor market may be defined less by specialized industry expertise and more by other strategic or organizational considerations. For example, a large consumer goods manufacturer suffering from a decline in market share might hire a CEO with a strong track record in turning businesses around from another large and equally complex, but unrelated, manufacturing organization. Similarly, a storage device company with an aggressive acquisition strategy may look to hire a new CFO or CHRO from an unrelated computer hardware company with a long history of corporate transactions, rather than recruiting from a direct industry competitor that has relied exclusively on organic growth.

- *Capital markets.* The capital market is made up of companies that an organization competes with for equity or other capital. These companies tend to share similar financial characteristics and risk profiles, and while the competition for investors can exist within a single industry, it may be broader. A large chemical manufacturer, for example, would compete with other large chemical companies, but also potentially with a wide range of other blue-chip manufacturers for investment dollars. Capital market peers can be identified by reviewing analyst or bond rating reports, or through analyzing stock price behavior to pinpoint other companies that investors view as having similar risks. Capital market peers are touchstones for evaluating your own company's pay-performance alignment since they most closely reflect organizations against which performance comparisons can be made.

These three markets usually overlap to a greater or lesser degree (Exhibit 6.2)—companies that compete in one of these markets most often compete in the others as well, with the best peers sharing all three markets. However, this is not always the case, so it is important to consider all three markets when evaluating whether other companies can be considered your peers.

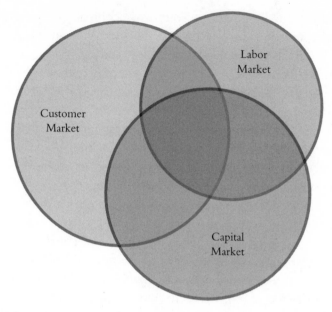

Exhibit 6.2   Competitive Markets of Peers
SOURCE: Mercer.

Analyzing peers from a variety of market perspectives is critical both when you have a large universe of peers to choose from and when available peers are limited in number. If your business operates in an industry characterized by many comparably sized competitors, you can apply multiple market perspectives to help filter out the very best peers. Conversely, if your business operates in a highly consolidated industry or within a small geography, a multifaceted approach to defining the competitive market can help you expand the number of potential peers.

Screen by Size

When it comes to executive remuneration, pay levels are strongly correlated with the size of a company. This is because larger companies, in general, manage more capital and have more complex operations, which means that their top executives have jobs with broader scope and greater responsibility.

Once you have identified peer group candidates based on the market competitive screens discussed above, you can narrow the field by choosing those similar to your own company in size. For most companies, revenue size is a reliable measure of complexity; for some, such as financial services, asset size is more indicative.

In the United States, executive pay typically increases 10 to 20 percent for every doubling of company size. Given this relationship, the peers you select should, as a general rule of thumb, range from one-half to twice the revenue (or assets) of your company, which should fall close to the median of the group. This guideline should be balanced with other important considerations, such as the unique character of your business and the number of available competitors.

Some companies use market capitalization as the primary size criterion in selecting peers. While there is a general correlation between the value of a company's outstanding equity and its executive pay levels, market capitalization is a volatile metric. It is strongly affected by expectations of future value and may not accurately reflect the size and scope of current business operations. A company's stock price may bounce around even when its overall character, complexity, and asset value have not changed; thus, companies selected based on market capitalization tend to come into or fall out of your peer group more quickly than companies selected based on revenues or assets. In Exhibit 6.3, using revenue criteria to identify peers for companies in the chemicals industry resulted in an average of nearly 9 in 10 peers selected remaining in the peer group two years later, whereas using market capitalization resulted in an average of one-third of peers falling out of the peer group two years later.

Maintaining consistency in the peer group composition over multiple years enables a company to develop a more accurate picture of market practices and to identify emerging trends. It also provides a defense against a common criticism of peer comparisons—that peer groups are changed annually to get the best results from benchmarking. Because the potential volatility in market capitalization could require frequent revisions to peers, it may best be used as a secondary screen to revenue or asset size.

Screen by Business Character

All else being equal, it is important to consider the character of the business when selecting a peer group. By character, we mean factors

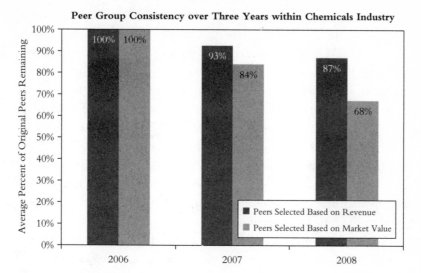

Exhibit 6.3   Revenue versus Market Capitalization as Peer Criterion
SOURCE: Mercer.

that relate to a company's business model, operations, or organizational structure.

Business model considerations might include the value proposition to customers or the distribution channels utilized. For example, an information technology organization that places a heavy emphasis on services may have more in common with a large consulting organization than an electronics manufacturing organization. Similarly, a cosmetics retailer that utilizes a direct distribution strategy may have more in common with other retailers using a direct distribution model than with a traditional cosmetics producer that distributes to independent retailers.

Factors related to operating character, such as asset intensity or the degree of outsourcing, may also impact peer fit. Two hotel chains, for example, might operate in similar markets and have comparable revenues. However, if one owns all of its properties and the other only leases or operates its hotels, the character, of the businesses are distinctly different, as are the risks. Executive pay would tend to be more highly leveraged in the riskier, asset-intensive company, making this distinction an important criterion in selecting peers. Another example can be found in the

semiconductor industry, where some companies both design and manufacture circuits, while others focus exclusively on research and development. The talent needs of these two types of companies will differ,
with the former requiring an executive team with greater expertise in
areas such as industrial engineering and procurement.

A company's organizational structure may also come into play.
Consider a large conglomerate with several autonomous business
units. The roles and responsibilities of the top executives in this type
of organization will vary significantly from those in a highly uniform
operating company. One executive team's rewards and program structure may focus more on business portfolio optimization while another
will be more operationally focused.

Peer group screening should account for these business character issues so that the ultimate group used is a fair comparator to your
organization. However, care also must be taken to eliminate otherwise
appropriate candidates that are undergoing extraordinary changes. The
elements of business character may point to a peer that is not appropriate based on these extraordinary circumstances. For example, this may
apply to companies that are undergoing dramatic business portfolio
changes or are in bankruptcy. In such cases, those organizations should
generally not be included in the peer group since they may not fairly
reflect "typical" pay practices.

Should Performance Be Considered?

With certain exceptions, it is best to avoid using financial or market
performance as a primary screening criterion when selecting peers.
Specifying "high performance" as a criterion—choosing companies
whose share price performance is in the upper quartile, for example—
is a good way to open your company to accusations of cherry-picking
peers to inflate your executive pay. It also potentially puts you in a logical bind. If you selected high performers because your company is also
a high performer, then you would be obliged to consider selecting a
new group of lower-performing peers if your performance wanes, as it
is likely to do—which would mean redesigning your pay program for a
lower set of expectations. The peer companies, too, are likely to experience performance volatility; a company that seemed to be a good peer
in one year might not set such a desirable standard in future years.

On the other hand, certain aspects of financial performance analysis can give you insights into the business character of a potential peer. A business's capital intensity ratio, profitability ratio, or valuation ratio (e.g., its price-earnings ratio) can be a clue that its business model or its perceived value to investors resembles yours. For example, pharmaceutical companies that invest heavily in the research and development (R&D) of new therapies tend to have higher price-earnings ratios than those that primarily manufacture generic drugs because the stock prices at R&D-focused companies are driven by future expectations regarding patentable products that will be able to command premium prices in the market. In this case, comparing price-earnings ratios across a group of potential peers could be a strategy for identifying companies with business models like your own.

As we have already stated, market capitalization is not an ideal metric for screening peers because of its volatility. However, comparative analysis of stock price movement can be useful as a way to identify companies whose executives deal with similar risk factors. Later in the chapter, we discuss how this type of analysis can be completed as part of the peer development process.

Desperately Seeking Peers

A company should have enough peers to get a statistically valid representation of the market. A coherent, well-chosen group of 10 to 15 is appropriate to balance the need for robust, meaningful data with the time and resources required to collect and analyze the data. If you have fewer than eight peer companies, outliers and aberrant data can skew your analysis. On the other hand, the administrative costs start to outweigh the returns when using too many peers—resulting in less-meaningful, less-targeted comparisons.

Identifying a sufficient number of peers can, in some cases, be a challenge. In highly consolidated industries such as health care or automobile manufacturing, in complex operations such as a diversified holding company, or in smaller geographic markets such as Canada and Australia, there may be few direct competitors and therefore a scarcity of comparable peers. Where there are only a few peers of similar size within an industry, a company should consider casting a wider net by taking a more comprehensive approach to peer group selection. Here are several different strategies that can be used to round out a limited peer group.

Use Quantitative Analysis to Uncover Capital Peers

While initial analyses may indicate that there are very few companies out there like your own, investors invariably compare the opportunities and risks presented by investing in your firm against the opportunities and risks of investing their money elsewhere. These comparisons, while not always obvious, tend to reveal themselves in stock market behavior, with the stock prices of companies exposed to similar external risks moving in concert over time.

As introduced above, one objective method for screening peers is based on the empirical patterns of comovement in stock price or *total shareholder return* (TSR). Performance Sensitivity Analysis® (PSA) puts this approach into practice by empirically estimating and isolating the comovements of stock prices that are caused by industry-related factors. This approach may identify potential peers that are overlooked in the initial screening process, which relies on more subjective judgments about what markets the company operates in. For more information about using PSA to select peers, see "Stock Price Analysis Reveals How Investors Group Companies."

Stock Price Analysis Reveals How Investors Group Companies

Changes in stock prices result from the decisions of investors based on how they expect various market and industry forces to impact future company performance. The stock price of companies that investors view as having similar risks will be influenced by externalities in like ways. These similarities can be uncovered by analyzing the stock price or *total shareholder return* (TSR) of companies over time for meaningful correlations.

Developments specific to an industry or sector will impact investor expectations for the future performance of that industry. After accounting for broader market movements, comovement among company stock prices or TSR reveal investors' judgments about the comparability of those companies and the risks they face. Put another way, those companies whose stock prices move more closely together can be regarded as stronger capital market peers than those whose stock price movements are more independent.

PSA puts this concept into practice by empirically assessing the comovements of stock prices that are caused by industry-related factors. The process begins with the collection of monthly stock price performance for the target company and a pool of potential candidates—typically a broad group of industry peers—over a three-to-five-year period. This data is then used to construct a time series of TSR for each company and, after adjusting for general market effects, correlations between the TSR of the target company and each candidate firm are measured. The size of the correlation indicates how closely the target company's TSR is associated with the TSR of different peer candidates. Finally, to ensure the correlations are meaningful and not caused by random errors, a statistical estimate of the likelihood of coincidence is calculated. If the likelihood of coincidence is low, we can be confident that the observed relationship captures the effect of industry fluctuations rather than pure coincidence.

One advantage of PSA is that it makes use of hard, factual evidence that can supplement the labor market, customer market, and capital market screens. This approach takes an investor-centric perspective. In addition to peer group selection, this approach can be used to validate a peer group that has been selected by more traditional means—it acts as an "investor check" on the results.

Focus on Business Character

While business character is often tied up with the primary screening criteria of markets and size, businesses from outside of your key markets can also be considered peers if they are like your business in other significant ways. If your company has few direct competitors, look beyond your customer, labor, and capital competitors for companies that manage comparable activities. For example, a large cable television company may have more activities in common with a telecommunication company of similar size than with a much smaller cable competitor. Both industries require heavy capital investment, seek to maximize revenue over a fixed capital base, and serve similar residential and business markets. Similarly, companies in the heavily consolidated health insurance industry share many operating characteristics with general insurance companies: both collect premiums from organizations and individuals, analyze and manage insurance risk, process claims, and provide customer service. Comparisons with companies outside of your primary markets may be appropriate, and even necessary, but should be done in a way that reflects sound judgment to support comparability with your company's situation.

Look Upstream and Downstream

Given the scarcity of executive talent, companies must often look beyond their traditional labor market for recruiting purposes. Companies in highly specialized industries may have to look upstream or downstream for managers who understand their operations, risks, and key metrics. For example, an executive in a chemical company that supplies a paper manufacturer probably understands the economics and operations of the paper business and can competently fill a job in that industry. In this case, these businesses may serve as valuable comparators when rounding out a remuneration peer group, even though they serve different markets.

Consider Global Competitors

In some highly specialized global industries such as mining there are simply not enough companies to allow meaningful country-specific comparisons. In cases where executive responsibilities routinely cross borders and the market for talent is truly global, it may make sense to construct a blended peer group that spans multiple geographies. The challenge with this approach, however, is that it can be difficult to get consistent pay and performance data given the varying practices and disclosure requirements in countries around the world. To make meaningful comparisons with a multinational peer group such as this, your company needs to make sure it fully understands and adjusts for these differences in the reporting of remuneration and financial data.

Peer selection is not a cookbook exercise, but like the best cooking, it is part science and part art. The science is in the numbers. Size, revenues, assets, industries, and stock price behavior are measurable means of direct comparison and analysis, and in many cases can provide most of the basis for selecting a representative group of companies that share important characteristics. On the other hand, if there are too many similar companies to form a compact, manageable set of benchmarks, you have to decide which ones to leave out, and if there are too few, you have to choose others from different groups that are not as closely related. The art is in applying experience and judgment to identify a practical, appropriate, defensible group of peers.

When One's Not Enough

A single peer group of 10 to 15 companies is considered ideal. However, there are situations in which you might find it useful, even necessary, to establish another peer group as a parallel standard for comparison. There may be circumstances where there are insufficient peers because of consolidation in an industry. Or, there may be cases where the company's business character does not squarely fit within one industry group. In those cases, a secondary peer reference may be appropriate. As in supplementing your direct competitors, subjective judgment plays a major role in deciding to form a secondary peer group.

The relevance of particular peer groups depends on the context in which they are being used. Generally, peers used to assess pay magnitude should be similar in size and complexity, while peers selected based on primarily market relevance or like business characteristics can be used to inform program design or performance target setting. We discuss five specific situations in which the use of a secondary peer group may be warranted below.

Supplementing a Limited Number of Direct Peers

If you've applied all the usual strategies to round out a peer group and yet have not been able to develop a sufficiently large sample, you may need to adopt a secondary peer group to validate the results of the core peer group analysis. For example, U.S. Fortune 50 companies, because of their sheer size and complexity, tend to have few direct competitors. In addition to benchmarking remuneration against a small group of industry peers, a company might use a general industry subset of the Fortune 50 as a check on whether the industry's pay levels, and by extension their own, are reasonable in light of company performance and shareholder expectations.

Mitigating Aberrant Data

A core peer group that is highly diverse or that exhibits unusual characteristics may produce results that show poor correlation or are obviously out of line with your company. Rather than base remuneration decisions on suspect data, it may be useful to draw parallels with a secondary peer group whose pay practices appear more in the mainstream. For example, if your core peer group consists primarily of newly public companies where the executives are also founders of the business, the resulting benchmarking data may be influenced by the relatively high ownership levels of these individuals. Assuming your executive team is made up of external hires, a supplemental peer group of more mature companies could provide benchmark data that are more relevant to your business stage and talent strategy.

Implementing a Change in Business Model

A company undertaking a major strategic shift will want to initiate a corresponding evolution in the peer companies used for remuneration and performance comparisons over time. One way to accomplish this is to form a new, or secondary, peer group of companies that resemble the business it is moving into. For example, a computer manufacturer entering the professional services field might soon find itself competing with other professional services companies for executives who are hired to transform the company and execute against the new strategy. A secondary peer group of technology-focused professional services firms could be identified and used alongside the old peer group until the transition in business strategy is completed.

Designing Remuneration Packages

Normally, a single peer group is used as a yardstick for all pay practices. In some situations, however, a company may find that one peer group is instructive for setting overall pay levels, while another set of peers provides more useful insights into the different parts of a remuneration program, such as long-term incentive delivery. For example, a software company that is significantly smaller than its direct competitors may use a peer group of similarly sized companies in the broader high-tech industry to set reasonable remuneration levels given the size and scope of the business. However, in deciding the proportion of remuneration to deliver in cash and equity or what performance metrics to use in its short-term incentive plan, the company might find advantage in looking to the practices of larger direct competitors.

Setting Incentive Plan Targets

A supplemental or expanded peer group may help a company set effective incentive plan performance targets or may be used to measure relative performance results with greater meaning. For example, a large national retailer may benchmark its remuneration practices against other similarly sized retailers or other large general-industry companies of similar scale, but may consider using a broader range of retailers when setting performance goals or measuring results since these companies are subject to similar external market dynamics and represent a formidable competitive challenge to the market position of the company.

Multiple peer groups can help inform the design of a competitive remuneration program, but a well-defined process should be established to determine how the peers are selected and how the multiple groups are used in pay decision making. For example, one peer group may be designated as a "primary" reference while others are secondary checks on the primary data. In other cases, a blend of all peer groups may be utilized, or pay may be assessed each pay group separately with good judgment used in reaching decisions. For public companies in the

United States, disclosure rules require a discussion of how peer groups are utilized in the pay decision-making process. So, care should be taken to ensure that the company can explain their use.

Using multiple peer groups can be very powerful. Certainly, market data should not be used selectively to support foregone conclusions, and the process must be fully transparent to shareholders—particularly if your company uses different peers for remuneration and performance comparisons. However, assuming care has been taken to mitigate the possibility of manipulating peer data, the additional information that comes from multiple peer groups can provide new ways of looking at your company's pay program, offering you greater insight into how to effectively motivate and reward your top executives.

Maintaining Peer Groups

Your business changes over time, as does that of your peer group members. How frequently should you reexamine peer groups to see if they are still valid? This decision comes down to a balance between consistency in year-to-year measurement and the risk of going stale over time.

Generally, a company should take a close look at its peer groups approximately every three years unless either your company or its peers experience a significant change in business strategy or corporate restructuring activity. Examples of circumstances that might give rise to an interim review of peers include material change in business portfolio, merger and acquisition activity, new business competitors, or significant change in business economics. In the absence of these changes, more frequent peer group examination can result in undesirable inconsistencies in year-to-year analyses and, potentially, may open your company to accusations of manipulating outcomes. Conversely, if you wait five years or longer to reevaluate the peers, particularly in a fast-changing business climate, your pay levels and practices may become outdated and uncompetitive.

Peer Groups in Practice

Peer groups provide an objective basis for decisions involving three remuneration parameters: pay magnitude, program design, and performance alignment. A thoughtfully selected peer group is one of the most critical steps in the executive remuneration decision-making process. Peer group comparisons can help to make sure that your company's pay practices are competitive and reasonable relative to performance results. This can help ensure that you attract, motivate, and retain the executive talent needed to execute your business strategy. These comparisons also provide external validation to the board of directors and shareholders that pay actions are responsible.

This book is concerned mainly with how companies design pay programs that effectively link pay outcomes to performance so companies can make the most of pay as a management tool. In today's information age, benchmark remuneration information is available through a variety of sources—published remuneration surveys, recruiters, and even Web sites. But peer group public disclosures remain the best source of both remuneration and performance data, and analyzing both types of information in combination can help ensure that a company's remuneration programs reasonably and competitively reward executives for the results they achieve.

Remuneration data for the CEO, CFO, and next three highest paid executive officers are reported in the annual proxy statements of public companies in the United States. These companies must report not only the total amount of remuneration received, but must also provide detail on the rationale for *why* the disclosed level of pay was delivered. Primary among the "why" factors is performance—both company performance and individual executive contributions if they are used in the pay determination. Companies need to be prepared to explain both *what* they reward for—in other words, what performance measures are utilized— and *how much* performance achievement was required to earn the payouts disclosed. Peer groups can be used to help with this disclosure.

Detailed financial performance information can be collected from the quarterly and annual financial statements of peer companies, or through subscription services that aggregate this information for investors. Additional information that can help make sense of financial or market results can often be found in analyst reports, including predictions for the industry or analysis of relevant economic trends.

Remuneration and financial information can be analyzed together to determine whether the relative positioning of your company's executive remuneration program—in terms of base salary, short-term incentives earned, and value accumulated in long-term incentives over time—aligns with your company's performance relative to peers in the short-term and over a longer period. For instance, how do your shareholder returns stack up against those of your peers? Are you paying your CEO at the 25th percentile level for results that rank in the 75th percentile?

By analyzing the relationship between pay and performance at your own company and among peers, you can validate whether or not your remuneration program is effectively rewarding performance results. If you discover a misalignment, additional research on peer group practices may help you to better understand why. For example, if your short-term incentive payouts appear high relative to corporate performance on key financial metrics, you might conduct a more detailed examination of the incentive programs used by your peer group for clues. Are you evaluating performance using different metrics than your peers? How does the minimum level of performance required by peers to earn an award compare to your own? The answers to questions such as these can often help you fine-tune your own program design for better results.

In addition to measuring the alignment of pay and performance after the fact and enhancing program mechanics, peer company pay and performance data can also be used in the annual target setting process or as performance criteria under a relative performance plan. For example, a company that uses earnings growth as a performance metric under its long-term incentive plan could conduct a probability analysis of various outcomes using historical earnings growth data from peers. This probability analysis can help inform the likelihood of achieving specific three-year earnings growth targets, which in turn could help your company decide where to set threshold, target and maximum performance criteria.

What's Next?

In Chapter 7 we explore the use of peer group data in setting performance targets, as well as the advantages and pitfalls of comparing performance directly against peers in a relative performance plan.

Chapter 8 introduces various strategies for calibrating pay and performance, many of which involve comparative analysis against peers. Both goal setting and pay and performance calibration rely heavily on peer group data and the value of such information depends on the relevance of the peer group to your organization. Peer group selection is a critical building block for making responsible executive remuneration decisions. All companies should invest the necessary time to develop a cohesive, relevant peer group—and to discuss how data collected from this group can be used to improve linkages between executive pay and business performance.

Chapter 7

You Don't Need a Crystal Ball

Taking the Guesswork Out of Target Setting

T he performance measurement framework must signal to executives the financial and strategic priorities of the company to help direct their efforts toward the most critical actions. But it is not enough to decide you want executives to grow market share or improve returns—you must determine by how much. Performance metrics need to be translated into specific, measurable targets at the beginning of each performance period—an activity that many companies struggle with year after year.

The key is to set goals that are challenging enough to meet shareholder expectations, but achievable if the executive team performs competently. Set goals unrealistically high and executives may get discouraged and abandon their efforts. Set goals too low and executives have little incentive to take advantage of significant opportunities.

This concept seems simple enough, but how can you determine what is good performance before the results are in? Annual revenue growth of 5 percent may represent mediocre performance in a booming economy, but the same level of growth may be outstanding during a period of economic recession. Further complications start to build when you raise other issues:

- To what extent are the results attributable to actions by the executive—that is, would the outcome have been the same no matter who was behind the desk?
- How much better might the results have been had the executive fully realized the company's potential?
- To what extent did the executive just get in the way of achieving the results?
- How much better or worse did the executive perform than the average executive?
- How did the results compare with those of your company's peers?

As you can see, executives do not perform in a bubble. Performance is defined relative to the company's inherent potential, relative to other executives' accomplishments, and relative to the market as a whole. The only way to judge an executive's performance is in relation to other factors, whether internal, external, or both.

Therein lies the central question of this chapter: What is the best way to set the performance targets that determine incentive awards when the context for that performance has yet to unveil itself? You may not have a crystal ball to see into the future, but by incorporating a wide range of perspectives into the target-setting process, your company can develop well-informed targets against which executive performance can be confidently and fairly measured and rewarded.

What's Fair?

Paying for performance means more than simply establishing a relationship between company performance and executive pay. To demonstrate that what it pays its executives is appropriate and competitive, a company must be able to show that the amounts and types of compensation awarded are commensurate with the amount, kind, and value of results produced, and further leading to the increase (or decrease) in company value. In order to do this, the company must set performance targets—a set of benchmarks that determine the value of the incentive pay awarded. These benchmarks reflect a balance between shareholders' objectives and appropriate rewards for executive performance.

Like other aspects of designing executive compensation programs, setting performance targets is both science and art. The science involves doing the research into how internal or external factors might influence performance outcomes and competitive incentive awards; the art is in using insight, experience, and judgment to synthesize all of this information and develop targets that are fair to both executives and shareholders.

A "fair" goal will meet two sometimes conflicting objectives. It must be both:

- *Achievable.* A set of results that has a reasonably good chance of being realized.
- *Meaningful.* An outcome that results in increased shareholder value.

Finding the right balance between achievable and meaningful means walking the line between overpaying (thus incurring the wrath of shareholders and others) and underpaying (with the risk of damping the incentive to perform or losing the executive to another company). To further illustrate this concept, consider three possible outcomes of the target setting process:

- If targets are set too high—that is, if the goals are meaningful but perhaps not achievable—a sense of futility can set in early and motivation goes out the window. Unrealistically high goals can mean that executives end up getting paid less than their peers even if your company's performance is above the industry average.
- If targets are too low, executives may receive above-average incentives for mediocre performance. Potential red flags include consistently paying above-average incentive awards relative to industry peers for middle of the road performance or paying large incentive

payouts when the stock price is down. In this case, targets are achievable, but not likely meaningful.

- If targets are set at the right level, they will be meaningfully aligned with shareholder interests, and there will be similar likelihood of falling short of or exceeding the established goal. This puts the outcome squarely in the hands of the executives.

As a general "rule of thumb," a well-calibrated pay plan results in incentive payments at or above the target level about half the time (see Exhibit 7.1). Meanwhile, threshold levels typically have about an 80 percent probability of achievement, while maximum awards are earned less than 10 percent of the time. These definitions may vary somewhat depending on a company's unique compensation philosophy. For example, if the company's base pay is higher than the industry average, tougher targets may be appropriate for rewarding truly exceptional performance. We discuss calibration of award and performance levels in greater detail in Chapter 8.

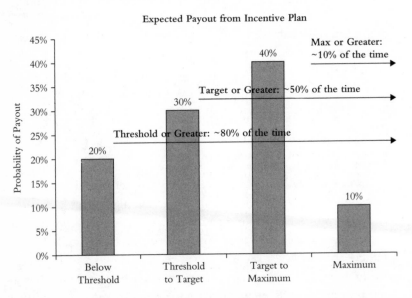

Exhibit 7.1 Probability of Incentive Award Payouts
SOURCE: Mercer.

Setting Performance Targets

Setting performance targets is one of the top concerns of directors when it comes to executive compensation. The reason it causes anxiety is that so many factors are in play: the demands of shareholders, the pressure to compete for executive talent, the vagaries of the marketplace, and innumerable financial and operational factors. A well-known principle of motivational leadership is setting goals that are a stretch, but not impossible to achieve: the higher the target—so long as it remains realistic—the better the results. The tendency of the participant, on the other hand, is to "sandbag"—keep targets low so that it's easier to exceed expectations—to generate larger incentive payouts. Between the sandbagging and the stretching lies a broad field of decisions strewn with potholes and tiger traps. Doubts assail directors at every step:

- If we expect less, are we being naive about how much could be accomplished? Are we paying handsomely for results that even a mediocre team could have achieved?
- If we expect more, are we being unrealistic? Are we holding the executive's remuneration hostage to an impossible goal?

Savvy directors strive to set targets that are ambitious but theoretically achievable. They like to challenge their executives—to keep them a little uncomfortable but not in despair—and they use a well-crafted pay package as motivation for the executive to outpace the average performer and stretch for the high bar.

But how do you know if a target has been sandbagged or if it is unreasonably high? While industry volatility and performance track records may be primary considerations for some companies, all organizations today are dealing with an ever-shifting marketplace and near-constant change. This requires a thoughtful, involved approach to goal setting using as much relevant information as possible to judge the degree of difficulty in attaining performance targets. Many variables influence how a company tackles goal setting, but companies typically approach goal setting from three perspectives, either alone or in combination:

- *Internal*, with absolute targets based on budgeting and strategic planning or upon other company-specific standards, such as the cost of capital. The factors in play in this approach all come from the company's own history, plans, and projections.

- *Externally informed*, with internally defined targets shaped by competitors' performance, shareholder expectations, and other external considerations.
- *Relative*, which sets targets based entirely on performance comparisons with peers.

All three approaches involve some subjective judgments based on objective data. The numbers, as usual, speak for themselves, but selecting the metrics and analyzing the output is an art informed by experience and judgment.

Internal Target Setting

Companies that set performance targets by the internal approach alone usually place great stock in their ability to measure and analyze their historical performance and use it as the principal basis for planning and predicting future performance. Having applied rigorous internal budgeting and planning processes that have already been scrutinized and approved by the board, they are confident they can set targets that are both meaningful and fair.

However, setting goals against purely internal objectives can lead to problems. Budgeted incentive payments may be made even when results don't correspond with expectations. These may be excessive when performance falls short, or they may fail to reward outstanding performance when results greatly exceed projections. Moreover, when only internal views are considered, management self-interest has undue influence. Expectations are more readily subject to sandbagging—that is, the most prominent voices being heard include those of the executives who stand to benefit if expectations are set artificially low.

Internally driven goal setting can easily fail to recognize and incorporate shareholder expectations and so may not be meaningful in terms of creating value for shareholders. This can sometimes be the case among organizations that take a purely "bottom-up" approach to goal-setting, where various business units and functional groups develop budgets related to their specific area of oversight that are then rolled up to set corporate-wide goals. If the sum of the individual pieces does not match shareholder expectations for the business as a whole, the stock price will inevitably fall over time—even if the internal targets are met year after year.

Focusing too heavily on a company's internal context can also result in a less nimble and dynamic organization. In years of strong industry performance, internally focused expectations can hobble a company's ability to take advantage of unforeseen market opportunities for growth and profit. Conversely, during a market downturn, executives may be led to make rash decisions that prop up short-term results, such as selling off assets, inadvertently affecting the viability of the business over the long term.

Given these limitations, setting targets purely from an internal perspective has been falling out of favor in recent years. By uncoupling the budgeting process from target setting for incentive plans, companies can reduce the pressure on the budget setting process and, in turn, increase the likelihood that executives will provide fair estimations of the future potential of the business. Supplementing internal estimations with externally derived data, such as historical peer performance, can also improve the credibility of performance targets in the eyes of shareholders by bringing a greater sense of objectivity to the process. We discuss two different ways to incorporate external data into the target setting process in the next section.

Externally Informed Target Setting

Incorporating outside information such as prospective industry performance, shareholder expectations, and peers' or competitors' performance, the externally informed approach to target setting builds on a company's budgeting and strategic planning but factors in other standards and influences. Historical performance is used to gauge budget accuracy, and the strategic plan provides a basis for projecting future performance. In addition to these inputs, the company may consider a range of external factors, including:

- *Industry analysts' expectations.* Analyst expectations for the industry as a whole, and your own company, can be used to assess the degree of difficulty built into performance targets. Most industries have reliable data, but it is important to use analysts who do independent research rather than relying on management to supply (and perhaps bias) the relevant data.

- *Macroeconomic indicators.* These are useful for gauging the growth of future demand for products or services in specific economies. For example, if a company operating in China budgets for 10 percent annual growth but the Chinese economy is expected to grow 20 percent per year, the company's performance targets may need to be raised.
- *Historical and predicted performance of industry peers.* Analysis of information about competitors and peers can help predict industry trends that will affect your company's growth and performance. In the case of externally informed goal setting, the use of peer performance relies on information and judgment versus rigorous peer-to-peer comparisons.
- *Explicit shareholder expectations.* Talk with shareholders to find out what they expect the company to achieve and their ideas on how it should achieve those goals. If shareholders expect 12 percent growth and see only 10 percent as a target, the stock price may fall.
- *Implicit shareholder expectations.* Rigorous analysis of a company's market capitalization can improve understanding of the long-term financial performance needed to justify current share price, as well as the level of performance required to add shareholder value (see Exhibit 7.2). As discussed in Chapter 5, this type of analysis can help you determine if your business plan will generate sufficient future cash flows to make up the difference between the value of your current operations and your market value, thereby verifying whether or not your incentive plan targets are meaningful.

Externally informed target setting has come into widespread use because it combines the strengths of rigorous internal planning with the value of outside information about markets, competition, the industry, and overall economic conditions. It requires more research than the purely internal approach and a lot of subjective judgment about what information is relevant and how it should be used, but if applied appropriately, the externally informed approach gives a more complete and accurate prediction on which to base realistic performance targets.

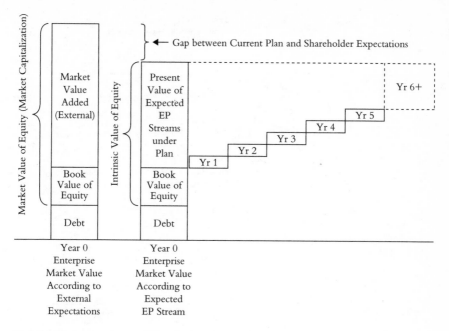

Exhibit 7.2   Analysis of Shareholder Expectations
SOURCE: Mercer.

Setting Performance Targets Using an Externally Informed Approach

Here's a step-by-step example of how absolute performance targets might be set using an externally informed approach. The objective is to gather as much information as possible relevant to your industry's recent performance, external and internal projections of your company's future performance, and the performance of your peers. To help process the information visually, a payout curve is constructed on a graph showing the selected metric—in this case, *return on invested capital* (ROIC)—on the X axis and the award (as percent of the target amount) on the Y axis.

Begin by entering internally collected ROIC data along the X axis of the graph shown in Exhibit 7.3. Your company's average ROIC for the past three years has been 9 percent; preliminary budgeting positions ROIC at 10 percent for the current year. Your cost of capital, however, is 13 percent, so the goal is to gradually increase ROIC until you are

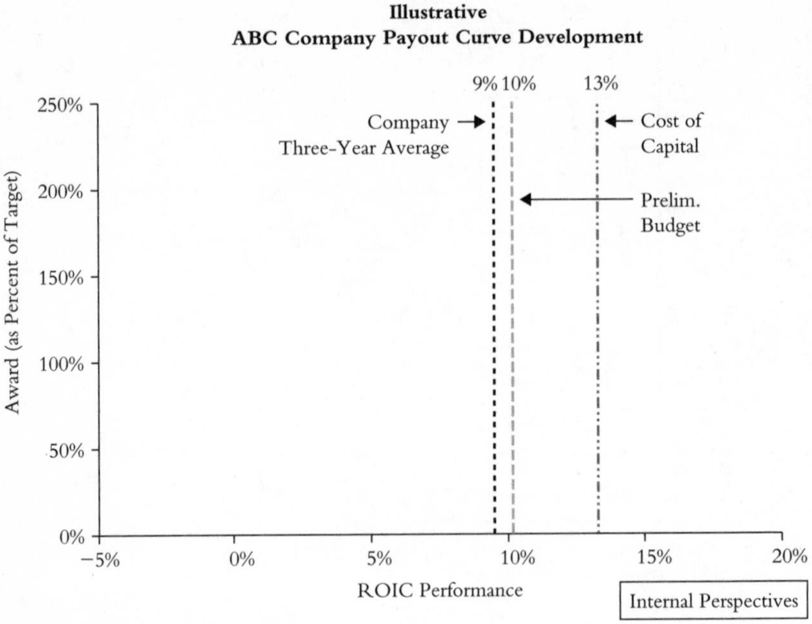

Illustrative
ABC Company Payout Curve Development

Exhibit 7.3   Internal Perspectives Used in Externally Informed Target Setting
SOURCE: Mercer.

covering and surpassing that cost. If using an internal target setting approach, you would set your targets based solely on this information. However, in an externally informed target setting approach, the internal data are supplemented with a variety of external reference points.

The next step is to collect historical ROIC data for your industry (in Exhibit 7.4). These data show that median ROIC for the preceding three years was 11 percent, with 3 percent being the first quartile and 16 percent marking the third quartile.

Finally, consider how people on the outside think your company will perform, and how the industry as a whole will perform, in the coming period. In the example shown in Exhibit 7.5, Wall Street analysts think your company will realize a ROIC of 8 percent, slightly below the expected industry average. In addition, analysts expect industry returns to double over the next three years, to 18 percent.

All of these internal and external data come together in the final graph, shown in Exhibit 7.6, to help you delineate your payout curve. Where should the performance target be set? That is, at what level

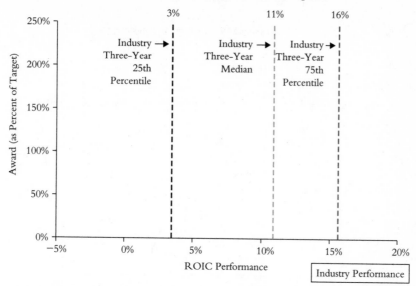

Exhibit 7.4   Historical Industry Performance Used in Externally Informed Target Setting

SOURCE: Mercer.

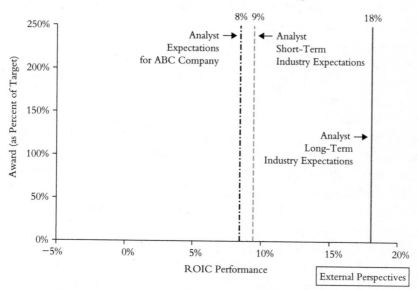

Exhibit 7.5   Analyst Expectations Used in Externally Informed Target Setting

SOURCE: Mercer.

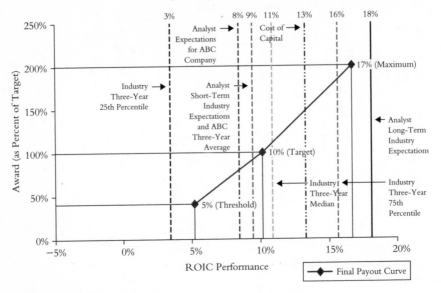

Exhibit 7.6 Payout Curve Derived Using Externally Informed Target Setting
SOURCE: Mercer.

of ROIC do you pay out 100 percent of the incentive award? Your three-year company average is 9 percent; the analysts' forecast for your industry is 9 percent (although they expect your company to come in at 8 percent). You need to be improving, so you finalize your performance target at 10 percent, which is where you will pay 100 percent of the target incentive award opportunity.

Now, what level of performance should be required to earn the maximum payout level? In order for your executive to be paid the maximum—twice the target amount—you decide that your company's ROIC should be in the top quartile of your peers. Historically, that's been 16 percent, but analysts expect the industry average to reach 18 percent in a few years, so somewhere in that range—say, 17 percent— seems to be a good place to anchor your maximum incentive award.

On the low end, you decide you don't want to fall into the bottom quartile, where the ROIC has been 3 percent. You know the industry is projected to improve, so you plot your threshold award level, 40 percent of target, at 5 percent—and you will pay no award if your ROIC is below that level.

Incorporating a variety of factors—internal and external, historical and prospective—into the target setting process helps ensure that incentive payouts will be commensurate with performance levels. The additional rigor can also improve transparency for shareholders, giving them greater confidence in the decision-making processes used to determine incentive awards.

Relative Target Setting

The rising acceptance of the externally informed approach comes largely from the recognition that the external environment plays a major role in the success of any effort to raise shareholder value. Even the best efforts of the most talented executives may not be enough to keep a company growing and profiting in a general market downturn or an industry-wide shakeup.

The environment can vary not only over time, but also across borders. For example, one multinational company found that the incentives paid to executives in certain countries averaged far higher year-to-year than in other countries (see Exhibit 7.7). Were the highly paid executives in Russia performing exceptionally well? Were those in other

		Incentive Payout Percentages by Country/Region						
		Overall Payout (%)					Five-Year Average	Percent of Time at 100%+
	Country/Area	Yr 1	Yr 2	Yr 3	Yr 4	Yr 5		
Above 100%	Russia	185%	135%	179%	170%	136%	161%	100%
	Australia/New Zealand	168%	105%	160%	173%	181%	157%	100%
	Central/Eastern Europe	176%	140%	156%	131%	109%	142%	100%
	China	185%	136%	160%	86%	145%	142%	80%
	Czech Republic/Slovakia	157%	122%	150%	132%	126%	137%	100%
Below 100%	Mexico	97%	72%	93%	65%	60%	77%	0%
	Spain	104%	45%	30%	97%	21%	59%	20%
	Chile	25%	16%	30%	68%	77%	43%	0%
	South Africa	86%	16%	30%	18%	21%	34%	0%
	France	25%	16%	30%	18%	21%	22%	0%

Exhibit 7.7   Example of Incentive Payout Percentages by Region
SOURCE: Mercer.

countries, such as France, consistently underperforming? Closer examination showed that the incentive payments were the result of faulty target setting that rewarded ordinary performance in countries where overall economic growth made everybody look like a star performer, while penalizing good performance in countries where the economy was more sluggish. The company needed tougher performance goals in Russia and Australia, less strenuous targets in France and South Africa—a problem it eventually solved by adding market share as a performance metric.

The company found market share to be a useful metric because it essentially measures performance relative to competitors. If your market share goes up, the market share of your competitors must have gone down. By measuring performance on a relative basis, the company was able to more accurately assess business results in light of country-specific economics.

Using a relative measurement approach does not require that you use an inherently relative metric like market share. Performance results can be compared against the results of peers on a wide range of market and financial measures. Consider a company where annual revenue growth dropped from 8 percent to 3 percent, but most of its competitors experienced a decline in revenues. Or perhaps revenues increased 30 percent, but one competitor folded and others picked up the bulk of the orphaned customers and averaged 65 percent sales growth. Evaluating performance by making direct comparisons against peers would reveal that the management team in the first example should be lauded for preventing a worse decline, while the second apparently failed to take full advantage of a big opportunity.

Conceptually, relative performance plans are pretty simple. Exhibit 7.8 illustrates a typical step payout schedule for a company with 10 peers in the group against which it measures performance results. If the management team lands the company squarely in the middle of the pack in terms of performance, it earns 100 percent of the target incentive. A ranking of third in EPS growth would earn 160 percent, eighth would net 60 percent, and so forth. One built-in virtue of this system is that any improvement or decline in relative performance is appropriately and automatically rewarded. A fall from top ranking, where the incentive payout is 200 percent, to the median results in a 50 percent cut in incentive pay, whereas bringing the company from eighth place to fifth, whatever

EPS Growth versus Peers (Rank)		Payment as a Percent of Target
1		200%
2		180%
3		160%
4		140%
5		120%
6	**(median)**	**100%**
7		80%
8		60%
9		40%
10		20%
11		0%

Exhibit 7.8   Relative Target Payout Schedule with a Ten-Company Peer Group
SOURCE: Mercer.

the economic environment, doubles the incentive pay. Note that some companies would set the threshold for payout at a higher performance level, for example, at rank nine and below.

A variation on ordinal ranking is to design a step payout schedule or payout curve based on percentile ranking against a peer group or index. Percentile ranking may be preferable to ordinal ranking if there is a longer performance period or if there is a strong likelihood that the composition of the peer group might change because it can be applied to a peer group of any size. For example, if a peer group used for performance comparisons includes 20 companies at the beginning of the performance period, but two of the companies merge and the third is acquired by a larger firm, only 18 peers will remain at the end of the performance period. A payout schedule based on ordinal ranking would need to be revised to reflect this change in the composition of the peer group (or two additional companies would need to be selected to replace those lost), whereas you could just as easily calculate a percentile ranking with 18 peers as with 20.

Incentive awards can also be keyed to the spread between the company's TSR and the results of a constructed or published index. The construction of an index can be complex in that you must determine how to weight individual company performance. One option is to weight all of the companies equally. Another common approach is to weight companies based on their respective market capitalizations. For example, the S&P 500 index reflects the average performance of the 500 largest U.S. public companies weighted based on each company's current market value.

Although less common and generally more complicated than direct peer comparisons, another variation is to evaluate performance relative to market opportunities as measured by selected external indicators. For example, a construction company might evaluate growth results in light of regional economic statistics like the number of housing starts during the same time period. Or within the oil or coal industries performance might be assessed relative to external commodity pricing. Because this version of the relative approach can be complicated to administer, it is more likely to be used as a tool for discretionary adjustment at the end of a performance period rather than as a principal determinant of incentive payouts.

Many companies like the relative approach because it minimizes the potential for sandbagging and eliminates the need to undergo a complicated target setting process each year. There is less pressure to guess the right targets, because the focus is on how your company performs compared with external benchmarks rather than on whether the targets are too easy or too difficult. By directly using information from companies that share similar internal economics, macroeconomic factors, and customer markets to judge results, the relative approach captures actual performance in a true competitive environment.

Yet relative target setting is not a panacea. It still requires careful calibration of awards and performance levels. For example, while it may be desirable to have TSR in the top quartile of your peers, it is nearly impossible to sustain this level of performance over the long term, making this an unrealistically high benchmark. We discuss strategies for testing the calibration of awards and performance levels in Chapter 8.

Relative performance measurement may also be more suitable for some companies than for others. There are several peer and data-related requirements that must be met for relative target setting to be effective, as well as some practical issues that should be considered before adopting this type of plan.

Requirements of Relative Target Setting

Although the relative approach obviates the need for hard targets, it can be challenging to execute because it requires companies to have:

- *Peer group stability.* Rapid loss or turnover of peers from your company's peer group as a result of industry consolidation shrinks the number of peers available for benchmarking performance.
- *Timely data.* Few companies use the relative approach for annual incentive plans because comparable data are difficult to obtain and verify quickly. Your company may not see data from peers until several months after the close of their fiscal years, making timely performance assessment impossible. For this reason, relative target setting is generally better suited for multiyear performance plans.
- *Comparable data.* To use the relative approach, your company needs access to metrics from peers that are comparable to your own metrics. For example, if a company defines ROIC in a complex manner—say, capitalizing research and development investments or excluding construction in progress from invested capital—then ROIC may be extremely difficult or impossible to calculate for peer companies. Also, when comparing relative improvement rather than absolute results, calculated statistics can sometimes be misleading if the beginning value is negative or small. Consider one company that grows profits from $5 to $105 and a second that increases profits from $10,000 to $15,000. The first would realize an improvement of 2,000 percent while the second only improves profits by 50 percent. Still, it is difficult to argue that the first company performed better than the latter given the absolute results.

In addition to the technical requirements described above, there are other factors that should be considered before adopting a relative approach. If your company ranks high among your peers in a falling market, you must be prepared to pay, perhaps handsomely, for negative absolute performance. A sizeable award may certainly be justified if the management team has averted your peers' more serious declines. It can, however, be difficult to manage the message to shareholders whose investments have been directly hit by the drop in stock price.

Companies also need to be constantly aware of and ready to respond to changing external factors when using a relative approach. In a climate of rapid industry consolidation, your company should be ready to adjust quickly when peers disappear and data become more or less available. The telecommunications industry, for instance, has undergone multiple mergers, consolidations, and financial restructuring over the past few years, and peer groups in that industry today look completely different than they did just a few years ago.

Furthermore, some companies may be better suited to relative performance comparisons than others, particularly when using market-based metrics. As discussed in Chapters 5 and 6, a company's stock price volatility can be attributed to three categories of factors: market, industry, and company-specific. The effectiveness of traditional equity awards may be questionable among companies with high-levels of systematic risk—that is, companies whose stock price performance is highly sensitive to changes in the general market—because stock price fluctuations are largely dependent on factors outside of management's control. For these companies, relative performance comparisons can help isolate the portion of stock price volatility that is attributable to executive performance. On the other hand, there is already a strong line of sight between executive performance and stock price at companies with low levels of market and industry risk. For these organizations, using relative performance evaluation would provide little, if any, advantage.

Although the relative approach is a reliable and uncomplicated way to measure executive performance, it is not foolproof. Accordingly, many companies choose to use relative assessment in combination with other performance measurement approaches—for example, as part of an incentive program that uses three performance metrics but measures only one by direct comparison, or for making discretionary adjustments to payouts in years when results exceed plan but fall short of overall industry performance. Incorporating a variety of perspectives into the performance measurement process helps ensure a well-balanced incentive program.

No Simple Answers

In recent years, the trend has been away from purely internal absolute target setting and more toward an externally informed approach, and some companies are beginning to edge into the relative approach (see Exhibit 7.9). Mercer's research indicates that the target-setting method chosen depends largely on the segment of the compensation package under consideration:

- For short-term plans, about half of the companies studied are following a strong trend toward using the externally informed approach when setting annual incentive goals. Nearly 40 percent, however, still use the internal approach for this purpose; the remaining 10 percent use some form of the relative approach.
- For long-term, multiyear plans, nearly 45 percent use an internal approach, 30 percent an externally informed approach, and 25 percent a relative approach. Both the externally informed and relative approaches are trending slightly upward as companies rely less and less on purely internal measures.

These trend data show that, in response to the demand for greater transparency and accountability to stockholders, companies are relying more and more on external data and results relative to peers when designing compensation packages to reward their top executives for reaching and exceeding performance goals. In fact, many companies are choosing to use a combination of two or even all three of the

	Short-Term Plans		Long-Term Plans	
	Used by	Trend	Used by	Trend
Internal Absolute	35%	Strongly down	40%	Down
Externally Informed Absolute	55%	Strongly up	35%	Up
Relative	10%	Slightly up	25%	Slightly up

Exhibit 7.9   Relative Usage and Trends of Three Principal Approaches to Target Setting
Source: 2007 Mercer 350 Study.

basic target setting approaches outlined above in their short-term and long-term incentive programs to mitigate the potential biases and measurement challenges that sometimes plague each target setting approach individually.

Clearly, the market is moving in the right direction. No approach is perfect, but a well-balanced program—one that incorporates a variety of perspectives into the target setting process—can go a long way toward relieving the consternation and second-guessing that often surrounds this important activity.

In the next chapter, we take target setting one step further by introducing strategies for calibrating performance and award levels regardless of the target setting approach used. By constantly testing and fine-tuning your incentive plans, you can lend further credibility to the outcomes of your incentive award programs and ensure that they are properly motivating and rewarding executives for enhancing shareholder value.

Chapter 8

Passing the Big Test

Calibrating Pay and Performance

D espite the time and consideration invested in designing executive incentive programs, in the end, many companies—and sometimes the executives themselves—are surprised by the award payouts. Deciding on target levels for pay and performance can be a challenge, but anticipating the entire range of possible outcomes is even more difficult. Unfortunately, failure to fully understand the implications of your executive incentive programs can sometimes lead to startling results.

Performance criteria and corresponding award levels that seemed reasonable at the beginning of the performance period may no longer appear suitable given unexpected developments that significantly helped or hindered results. Or, while the payouts from a single incentive plan seem to be properly aligned with performance outcomes, the entire pay package—including salary, short-term incentive awards, and gains on equity awards—may be less easily justified. Further complications arise when considering remuneration over multiple years. Achievements that were rewarded in prior years may not prove sustainable, and remuneration accumulated over an executive's career may appear to be out of synch with business performance over the same time.

From a governance standpoint, boards need to understand exactly how incentive plans operate, at both anticipated and unanticipated performance levels. In order for the incentives to motivate the desired behaviors, executives, too, need a clear picture of what payouts they can expect under a variety of outcomes as they strive to meet specific targets. Additionally, to both control costs and limit unanticipated windfalls, shareholders, directors, and top executives will generally agree that limits need to be set on incentive payouts, even though the level at which they should be capped may be subject to vigorous debate.

To ensure that executive pay levels are correctly calibrated with performance, companies need to test the potential outcomes of their incentive plans under various scenarios and continually fine-tune the performance benchmarks and plan mechanics based on the findings. It is also critical to analyze potential outcomes for reasonableness in the eyes of shareholders, which means considering the portion of shareholder value creation that is shared with executives over time.

Incentive Plan Leverage

Calibrating incentive awards to performance results ensures that threshold, target, and maximum payout opportunities are appropriate for commensurate performance results. This usually involves building a certain amount of leverage into the incentive plan. Leverage describes the degree to which increases in incentive awards outpace improvements in performance; the greater the leverage, the higher the potential to receive significant awards for outstanding performance.

In an incentive plan with a *straight-line payout curve* (see Exhibit 8.1), the executive receives a small bonus when performance is below target, with payments increasing in exact proportion as performance improves. Bonus payments usually cluster in a narrow range, perhaps 50 percent to 150 percent of the target (i.e., 100 percent) payout. This is a

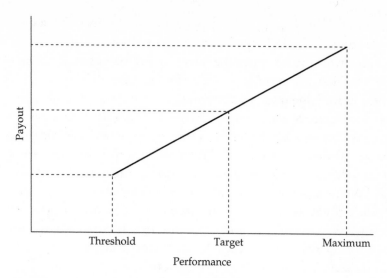

Exhibit 8.1   Straight-Line Incentive Payout Curve
SOURCE: Mercer.

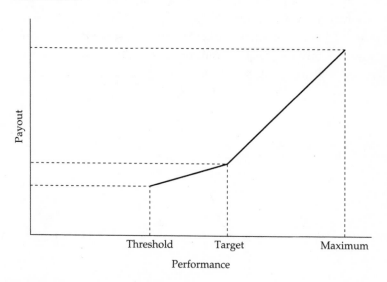

Exhibit 8.2   Kinked Incentive Payout Curve
SOURCE: Mercer.

common payout plan, particularly for mature businesses, but it is not appropriate for all companies.

In a more highly leveraged plan with a *kinked payout curve* (see Exhibit 8.2), the payout threshold may be closer to the target and bonus payments increase at a faster rate as performance exceeds the target. The executive incurs a greater risk of receiving no bonus, but he or she can also earn two to three times the target award for outstanding performance. This design is most appropriate for an easily scalable business where there is little downside to achieving better and better results.

Alternatively, an *S-shaped payout curve* (see Exhibit 8.3) is leveraged in a way that provides reduced incentive for falling near the plan threshold or maximum. This design gives executives additional motivation to reach target, but does not encourage them to "shoot the lights out." Where unfettered growth in one business area (for example, product sales) could negatively impact a company's ability to meet its objectives in other areas (like product quality or customer service), an S-shaped curve can help prevent reckless behaviors that could be detrimental to the overall health of the organization.

People will behave differently according to the degree of leverage you build into the pay program, so the shape of your incentive curve should compliment your business strategy. Is your company a startup, trying to carve out a substantial market share in a competitive market? Is it the kind of business, like consulting, that starts every year with essentially nothing and requires a strong show of entrepreneurialism

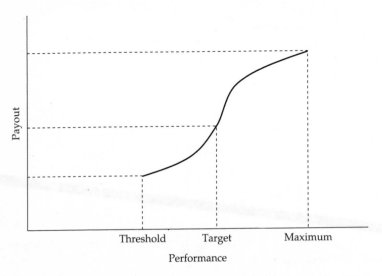

Exhibit 8.3   S-Shaped Incentive Payout Curve
SOURCE: Mercer.

from your team members to generate business? You need for your stars to shine. A highly leveraged incentive plan may be what you need to spur outstanding performances from your best people.

Conversely, is yours a stable, established business with a reliable base of long-term contracts? Or is your business only scalable to a certain extent, after which product quality or customer service delivery would likely suffer? Under circumstances like these, it may not be necessary, or even desirable, to motivate results that far exceed target performance levels. Your company would likely benefit from an incentive plan with less leverage and with the threshold and maximum payments closer to the target.

Highly leveraged incentive plans have traditionally been used to compensate individuals who have a very clear and measurable impact on performance results, such as sales professionals. They are also common among high-growth organizations, where the business strategy depends on outperforming the market, or among financial services companies like investment banks and private equity firms, where financial outcomes are very closely tied to individual contributions.

However, companies need to exercise caution when using highly leveraged incentive plans, as they may encourage excessive risk taking. In fact, uncapped, highly leveraged incentive plans focused on short-term financial results have been criticized for contributing to the speculative activities on Wall Street that eventually led to the financial meltdown. To ensure that results are sustainable, incentive plans should generally be capped at a reasonable level (which we discuss later in the chapter) and appropriately balanced with other, longer-term remuneration elements.

Another important consideration when building leverage into incentive plans is the extent of and manner in which executives influence the selected performance metrics. In industries like mining or petroleum, you have to be careful not to leverage incentives in ways that reward executives simply because the price of the resource went up. Measures that are strongly influenced by commodity fluctuations or other external factors outside of management's control may not be reflective of an executive's performance. Incentive awards based on these types of metrics, if used at all, should generally not be highly leveraged—unless, as discussed in Chapter 7, results can be accurately measured on a relative basis.

Leverage and Long-Term Incentive Vehicles

The amount of leverage contained in an incentive plan depends not only on the payout curve design, but also on the type of remuneration delivered. Share-based incentive plans, commonly used to reward longer-term performance, have a certain amount of built-in leverage that must also be considered in calibrating performance and reward levels.

Share-based incentive vehicles involve different risks and reward potential than cash-based incentive plans because the value earned is intrinsically dependent on share price performance. Exhibit 8.4 compares the leverage and performance orientation of several different long-term incentive types.

Stock options contain the greatest amount of leverage. Under a normal option award, if the stock price stays flat or declines, the option is worthless. On the flipside, stock options provide significant upside

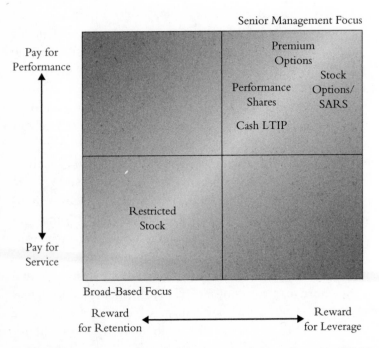

Exhibit 8.4   Comparison of Alternative Long-Term Incentive Vehicles
SOURCE: Mercer.

opportunity under positive share price performance scenarios, with the value of the option award increasing at a faster rate than other vehicles.

Restricted stock contains the least amount of leverage. The ending value of the award varies depending on share price but is less sensitive than an option award to share price volatility. If the share price declines, the restricted stock award retains some of its value, and if the share price increases, the value of the award also grows, but at a slower rate than a similarly valued grant of stock options.

Performance shares contain two types of leverage: (1) the leverage built into the payout curve that determines the number of shares earned, and (2) the leverage associated with changes in share price that determines the value of each share. Like the restricted stock grant, the shares retain some value even if the share price declines. However, the number of shares earned is subject to meeting specified performance criteria; if the threshold of the payout curve is not met, no shares will be vested and the executive earns nothing, regardless of share price performance. On the other hand, the executive often has the opportunity to earn additional shares, providing more upside potential than a restricted stock grant.

As with designing a payout curve for an annual incentive plan, the amount of leverage incorporated in your long-term incentive program should be an extension of your business and human capital strategies. What type of behaviors do you want to motivate? What is the appropriate balance between risk-taking and value preservation? How well have past long-term incentive awards retained executive talent?

Another key consideration is how well the performance metrics—meaning absolute TSR (total shareholder return) in the case of options and share-based awards—accurately reflect the performance of executives. If your company's TSR volatility is highly dependent on market or industry-related factors (as opposed to firm-specific factors, as discussed in previous chapters), a highly leveraged share-based incentive plan may reward or penalize executives for developments that are outside of their control. Such was the case with aggressive option grants awarded by U.S. technology companies prior to the burst of the dot-com bubble in 2000; many executives realized significant option gains driven by general market trends rather than by their company's actual performance.

Because long-term incentive awards extend over multiple years, it can be difficult to predict performance outcomes with a high degree of accuracy. This increases the potential for unexpected rewards earned by executives at the end of the performance period. Sustainability is also a concern; payouts that are quantified years in advance can be, or at least can appear, excessive in light of later performance downturns, whether caused by the market or by your company's own actions. For these reasons, it is critical that companies understand what executives stand to earn through long-term incentive awards and what the associated costs to the company might be at both anticipated and unanticipated performance levels.

Leverage and Goal Setting

One of the most challenging aspects of designing an incentive plan is setting appropriate performance targets. In the chosen metric, along the scale of possible outcomes, what value has both a reasonable likelihood of achievement and is sufficiently aggressive to drive the creation of shareholder value? This number typically becomes the performance criteria for paying 100 percent of the designated incentive award. It is usually based on an assessment of the company's prospects, derived from an in-depth analysis of environmental factors and internal and external projections, as described in Chapter 7. Similar considerations factor into setting performance benchmarks for threshold and outstanding award levels.

In addition to considering a wide range of external and internal inputs, it is advisable to test performance goals upon completion of the goal-setting process by estimating the probability of achieving threshold, target, and outstanding performance levels. This extra step helps to calibrate the amount of leverage in the incentive plan. Historically, the standard "rule of thumb" was considered to be that:

- Threshold goals would be achieved (and corresponding threshold awards earned) about 80 percent of the time.
- Target performance would be achieved about 50 percent of the time.
- Outstanding performance goals would be achieved about 10 percent of the time.

While performance-pay calibration differs from company to company, typically, achievement of threshold goals would earn 50 percent of target award opportunity, achievement of target goals would result in 100 percent of target opportunity, and achievement of outstanding goals would result in 150 percent or 200 percent of target opportunity.

A Mercer analysis of annual incentive award payouts captured in our annual Benchmark Database confirms these "rule of thumb" relationships. As shown in Exhibit 8.5, the analysis suggests a 79 percent probability of an award payout of 50 percent of target (which typically equates to a "threshold" performance goal); a 55 percent probability of an award payout of 100 percent of target opportunity; and an 18 percent and 7 percent probability of an award payout of 150 percent or 200 percent of target, respectively (typically equating to an "outstanding" level of performance).

In more highly leveraged incentive plans, the payout threshold and upside potential are increased and the probability of achievement may be less at all points along the payout curve. This relates a higher risk of

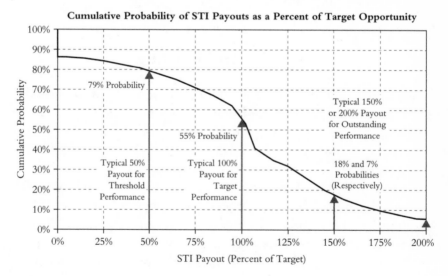

Exhibit 8.5 Cumulative Probability of Payouts of Short-Term Incentive Amounts

SOURCE: Mercer.

Note: The chart depicts the cumulative probability of short-term incentive payouts as a percentage of target aware opportunities for all incumbents (*n* = 36,000) with an articulated target opportunity in Mercer's Benchmark Database of remuneration data.

falling short of targets with the higher potential payout of achieving them. For example, the performance criteria for an "outstanding" award that is defined as 200 percent of target should have a lower probability of achievement than an "outstanding" award that results in a payment of only 150 percent of the award target.

The degree to which risk and reward are leveraged is a choice each company must make, based on its assessment of how it wants its executives to operate. However, whatever amount of leverage is desired, the company should be confident that the performance requirements are sufficiently aggressive to warrant the corresponding payout level and vice versa. As mentioned earlier, if the plan provides significant upside opportunity, companies should consider using a cap to ensure that awards do not reward excessive risk taking and remain within a reasonable range of competitive market practices. Alternatively, companies should consider ways to extend the time horizon of the plan—for example, by automatically deferring annual bonus amounts in excess of target into stock—so that executives are encouraged to take a longer view of performance.

Simulation Modeling

How does a company go about testing the leverage in its incentive plans? While past performance is not always a good indicator of future performance, the range of performance outcomes experienced over time can serve as a reasonable gauge for the likely range of outcomes going forward.

At the most basic level, you can estimate the probability of attaining certain performance levels by developing a probability curve based on historical observations of a company's (or a peer group's) financial or market results. The probability curve can then be used to test the relative difficulty of goals and to inform the payout curve design so that the desired amount of leverage can be achieved.

In Exhibit 8.6, a company's quarterly 12-month moving *return on capital employed* (ROCE) has been analyzed over a 10-year period to determine the likelihood of achieving certain performance levels. The cumulative probability of achieving 10 percent ROCE (or better) is

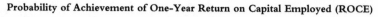

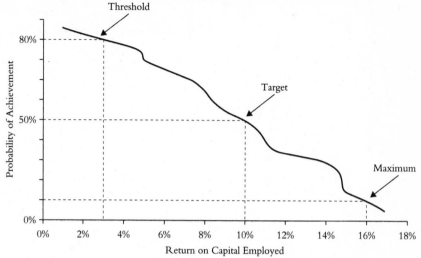

Probability of Achievement of One-Year Return on Capital Employed (ROCE)

Exhibit 8.6 Implied ROCE Performance Benchmarks Based on Cumulative Probability of Achievement
SOURCE: Mercer.

estimated to be 50 percent; in other words, over the past 10 years, the company has achieved a ROCE of at least 10 percent during approximately half of the performance periods analyzed. A 3 percent ROCE has an 80 percent probability, and at the high end, the probability of hitting the 16 percent ROCE is estimated to be 10 percent. Based on the "rule of thumb" guidelines discussed above, these ROCE levels would be considered reasonable performance benchmarks for threshold, target, and outstanding award levels (defined as 50 percent, 100 percent, and 200 percent of target, respectively).

By comparing these probabilities to the threshold, target, and outstanding performance goals identified during the company's annual target-setting process (see Exhibit 8.7), we discover that while the threshold and target performance levels appear reasonable, past performance outcomes suggest that the outstanding goal has a relatively high probability of achievement. One potential implication for the payout curve design may be that the outstanding award level be shifted downward to 150 percent of target to moderate the leverage in the plan. Alternatively, the company may choose to revisit the benchmark

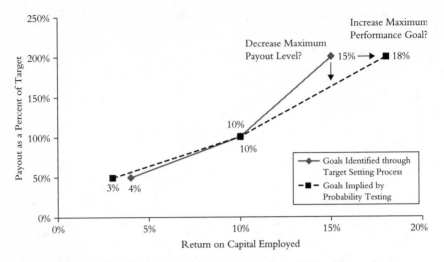

Exhibit 8.7 Comparison of Payout Curves Developed Using Target Setting Process and Probability of Achievement Analysis
SOURCE: Mercer.

set for outstanding performance to ensure that it is aggressive enough to warrant an incentive payment that is twice the target amount.

More complex modeling tools are also available to estimate the probability of various performance outcomes based on a greater number of variables. Monte-Carlo simulation, for example, runs thousands of iterations using different values for each of the variables identified. The results are then applied to create a probability distribution of outcomes that can be used to inform incentive plan calibration. This type of approach tends to be more reliable than the basic historical analysis described above, particularly for companies that operate in complex environments where measurable external factors have an observable impact on results.

Of course, companies should not rely solely on the rearview mirror when calibrating incentives. Simulation modeling based on historical data should always be balanced with forward-looking inputs, such as analyst expectations for the industry and management estimates of growth prospects for the near future. This is particularly important given the unprecedented nature of the current economic situation.

Simulation modeling can also be invaluable in designing share-based, long-term incentive programs. Estimating the value of share-based awards is important for budgeting and accounting purposes, as well as for communicating award levels to executives. In addition, a clear picture of the expected value and stock price sensitivity associated with various equity vehicles can help a company select from a menu of long-term incentive alternatives.

The first step to calibrating long-term incentive awards is to understand what the expected value of the award is on the date of grant. A number of tools are available for this kind of scenario testing based on historical stock price data. The Black–Scholes model is the most popular model for pricing options and takes into account the six primary factors that affect the value of the stock options: exercise price, current fair market value, volatility of stock, dividend yield, option term, and risk-free rate. The Binomial options pricing model is also common and is considered more accurate for longer-termed options and stocks that pay dividends because it uses a lattice approach to model the underlying variables over the life of the option, rather than a single point in time. When vesting is based on a relative performance measure, such as TSR, the Monte Carlo method is a more appropriate because it is based on considerably more variables than other valuation models.

Once the expected value of an option is determined, this information can be considered alongside other award characteristics, such as stock price sensitivity, to develop a long-term incentive approach that aligns with your unique business and human capital strategies. For example, suppose the Black–Scholes model tells you that the present value of an option is one-third the value of a share at the date of the grant. This means that in order to offer options with the same present value as full value shares, you would need to offer three times as many options as shares. Assuming that the fair market value on the date of grant is $10 and you want to provide the executive with a competitive long-term incentive opportunity equal to $20,000, you could grant 2,000 shares, 6,000 stock options, or some combination of the above (say, 1,000 shares and 3,000 options). Although the present value of each award would be equal at the time of grant, the actual value realizable by the executive is dependent on stock price performance (see Exhibit 8.8).

In this example, if the stock price stays below $15, the restricted stock grant will be worth more, but if share price rises over $15, the options will be more valuable because options are more sensitive to

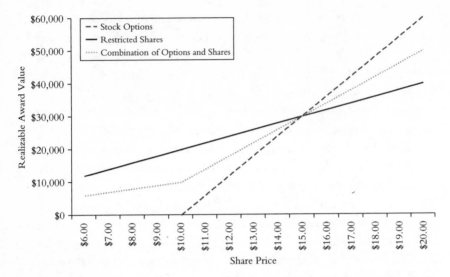

Exhibit 8.8   Value of Alternative Long-Term Incentive Awards under Various Share Price Scenarios
SOURCE: Mercer.

fluctuations in share price performance. If performance conditions are attached to the share awards, you would also need to factor in assumptions regarding the number of shares earned.

A high-growth startup may favor the use of stock options because the potential payout is high relative to the grant cost. For a more mature company, however, a less-leveraged long-term incentive program focused on restricted stock or performance shares may be preferable since full-value shares provide more consistent retention value under a wide variety of share price scenarios. No matter what your company's priorities, using simulation modeling to analyze alternative long-term incentive strategies under a variety of performance scenarios will help you to achieve the right balance between risk and reward.

Maximum Award Caps

Performance results and incentive payouts sometimes surprise both the company and the executive, not to mention the shareholders. To forestall unforeseen payouts and avoid unbudgeted costs, a company may consider ways to cap the maximum award that may be paid out under a variable incentive plan.

There are reasonable arguments both for and against caps. Without caps, the better executives perform, the more they can make, thus providing greater incentive for reaching or exceeding outstanding performance levels. But companies that offer incentives without caps run the risk of paying extremely high awards and may run into cash flow problems or face criticism from shareholders if remuneration levels fall outside of typical market practices. Uncapped incentives can also encourage shortsighted decisions or excessive risk-taking that could undermine the health of your business over the long term.

Most traditional annual incentive programs and cash-based, long-term incentive plans cap individual bonus awards by setting the maximum award level somewhere between one and a half and three times target. Some companies prefer to use a bonus pool tied to a measure of underlying profitability—for example, net income growth—to cap the total cost of the plan. An S-shaped payout curve (which shares less and less as performance levels increase) can be applied to either individual awards or bonus pool calculations as a further protection against reckless attempts on the part of executives to max-out the bonus.

Caps on annual bonuses or multiyear cash incentive awards are considered best practice for several reasons. The most obvious reason is that award payments directly impact a company's cash flow. Uncapped payouts resulting from unanticipated performance windfalls—particularly if the results prove unsustainable—could have a serious impact on a company's financial health.

In addition, if caps are not used and performance targets are poorly chosen, the incentive program might actually drive behaviors that can be detrimental to the company. The executive might be motivated to take unwise risks, or to focus entirely on the target metric and ignore other performance indicators, or perhaps even to manipulate other factors to achieve the targeted results destructively. By selling off a major blocks of assets, for example, a CEO might drastically cut costs and inflate profits, but at the cost of the company's future viability. In a well-balanced remuneration program, exceptional performance results that are sustainable will be rewarded in due time through equity appreciation or gain on other long-term incentive vehicles.

An alternative to capping cash incentive awards outright is to defer amounts in excess of a specified level. For example, some companies choose to pay annual incentives in excess of target or some other specified level in restricted shares. This way, the impact on cash flow is limited and the executive's final award amount is linked to share price over a longer time horizon.

Caps on long-term incentives most often take the form of limits on the number of shares granted. The value delivered to the executive through share-based grants may vary widely based on TSR, but the accounting cost per share is fixed up-front under most common equity plan designs. Thus, any share price appreciation or depreciation will not affect the cost to the company—resulting in a de facto cap, with a built-in limitation on share dilution.

The same holds true for performance share plans, where the number of shares earned by executives depends on performance against established benchmarks. For example, an executive may be awarded a target number of performance shares equal to one times salary, or $200,000. The target number of shares granted is determined based on the stock price at the beginning of the performance period; assuming the stock price is $20 per share, the executive would receive a target grant of 10,000 shares. These shares vest only upon the achievement of specified financial goals. If performance falls short or exceeds target, the number of shares vested may be adjusted up or down accordingly, but the cost per share would be fixed at the date of grant.

While the costs of share plans are capped, individual gains are not. Boards should be comfortable with the potential outcomes under all performance scenarios, including those characterized by significant stock price appreciation.

Assessing Plan Costs for Reasonableness

Every executive remuneration plan tries to provide a reasonable reward based on the overall results produced by executives. Thus, a key goal of any incentive plan is to ensure that the performance levels required for payouts align with shareholder results.

By testing the reasonableness of historical outcomes and potential future payouts, companies can improve both the directional alignment with and proportional relationship between executive remuneration and returns to shareholders. One way to do this is to conduct a cost-benefit analysis to quantify the relationship between shareholder value and the amount earned by executives.

Exhibit 8.9 shows the actual remuneration earned for the top five executives (defined as salary, actual bonus paid, and actual gain on long-term incentives) as a percentage of the increase in total shareholder value (defined as the total dividends paid plus the change in market capitalization) for a company and its peers over a three year period. Based on its comparative "TSR sharing ratio," the company can be confident that the proportion of shareholder value creation shared with executives is reasonable because it is well within the range of typical market practice for the industry.

Sharing ratios can also be used to forward-test the leverage contained in various incentive plan alternatives. Consider the example provided earlier, where the company was choosing between granting stock options, shares of restricted stock, or a combination of options and stock. By modeling out the estimated gain on these vehicles under

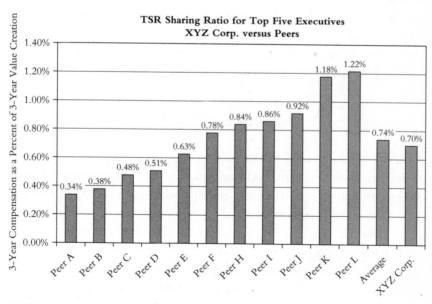

Exhibit 8.9 Three-Year Historical Sharing Ratio for XYZ Corp. and Peers
SOURCE: Mercer.

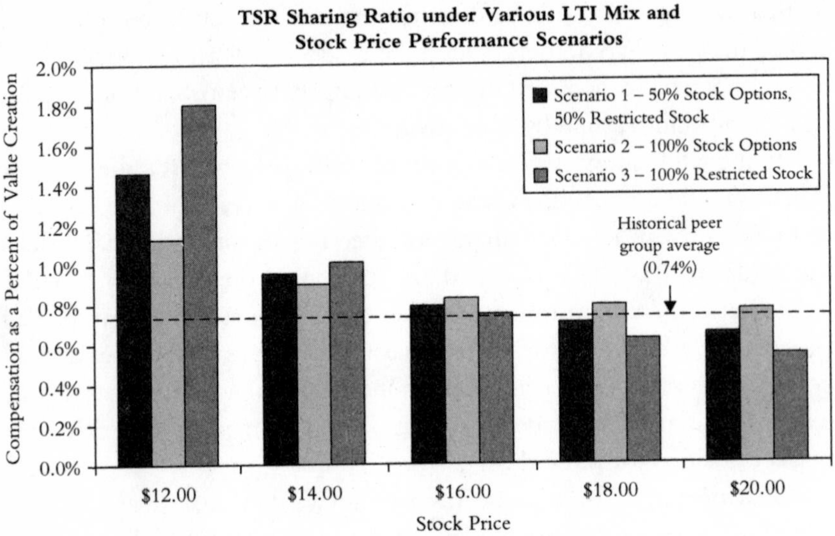

**TSR Sharing Ratio under Various LTI Mix and
Stock Price Performance Scenarios**

Exhibit 8.10   Implied Sharing Ratio under Various Stock Price Scenarios
SOURCE: Mercer.

various TSR scenarios and calculating the implied sharing ratio, the
company can get a better understanding of how sensitive the remuneration package is to market performance (see Exhibit 8.10) and make
adjustments to the long-term incentive mix to increase or decrease leverage as necessary.

Passing the Big Test

Successful calibration of incentive plans requires testing the entire range
of potential remuneration and performance outcomes and fine-tuning
the incentive leverage to achieve the optimal balance between risk and
reward. In addition, the testing and calibration process provides valuable
information that can be used for a variety of useful purposes.

Having a thorough understanding of plan mechanics and the likelihood of various award scenarios will enable your company to more
clearly communicate the economic opportunities provided to executives, greatly enhancing the motivational and retention value of your
incentive plans. Similarly, a comprehensive calibration process supports

a fact-based approach to decision making that helps prepare the board to explain incentive outcomes to shareholders, particularly in situations where remuneration might appear to be misaligned with share price appreciation or competitive market practice. From a more practical standpoint, simulation modeling can also help companies refine financial planning and cash flow projections and, in some cases, may be able to reduce accounting costs by more accurately estimating the value of equity awards.

Most importantly, however, these activities ensure that both the board and management have a mutual understanding of how the incentive programs operate and what remuneration outcomes can be expected under what scenarios. It is this understanding that provides peace of mind that there will be no ugly surprises lurking behind the next incentive award calculation or equity vesting date.

Chapter 9

Now What?

Avoid Managing by Exception

Throughout this book we have discussed strategies for designing an effective performance measurement and reward system, from selecting performance metrics to setting target goals to calibrating incentive plan leverage. Several key themes emerge. First, the performance measurement system should be a natural extension of a company's business strategy and must recognize its unique organizational character. Second, companies should take a comprehensive, fact-based approach to performance measurement design—one that uses research and quantitative analysis to inform decision making rather than relying on past experiences or untested beliefs. Finally, the performance measurement systems should be holistic in nature and should gauge financial and strategic results from a variety of perspectives.

Yet it is important to recognize that organizations do not operate in a vacuum. No matter how much care and consideration is invested in defining "good" performance or testing and refining incentive plan mechanics, all companies will confront measurement challenges from time to time. In addition, some organizations, such as those in highly cyclical industries or with recurring merger and acquisition activity, may face ongoing difficulties measuring performance in a volatile environment.

External events may impact business results in unanticipated ways. For example, financial results may be significantly helped or hindered by a natural disaster or an unforeseen change in the tax or legal code. In situations such as these, companies need to make decisions about whether to alter outstanding incentive awards, such as modifying performance targets, or whether to apply discretion to adjust incentive awards up or down to reflect the perceived value of performance results.

Business priorities can also change significantly in light of internal or external events. Companies can be acquired, enter into a joint venture with a competitor, or sell part of the business that is no longer central to its strategy. Ever-changing circumstances require an organization to adapt its business strategy to ensure the business remains successful. As the executive remuneration program needs to support the business strategy, it follows that some adjustments to incentive plans may be needed.

Despite the inevitability of changing conditions, there are ways that companies can be better prepared to meet performance measurement challenges. First, remuneration programs should be designed in a manner that provides flexibility in measuring performance under volatile situations. Second, incentive plan rules should be developed to address common measurement issues, such as how to adjust incentive plan goals in light of corporate transactions. Other situations may require case-by-case consideration, but decision making can still be guided by general principles identified and agreed to in advance in order to lend credibility to process in the eyes of both shareholders and incentive plan participants. Finally, the remuneration strategy should be reviewed every year or two for external competitiveness and strategic alignment with the business, with major organizational or strategic changes warranting a more hasty appraisal.

In this chapter, we examine several common issues that arise and discuss how companies can apply the strategies outlined above to deal with such situations in a consistent, fair, and defensible manner.

Designing Incentive Plans for Maximum Flexibility

The old adage "the best offense is a good defense" can be just as easily applied to the process of performance measurement as it can to the game of football. A well-designed remuneration program will go far toward eliminating the need to tinker with metrics or targets or rely on discretion to "fix" incongruous reward outcomes.

First and foremost, the incentive program must be well balanced so that the potential bias in any single measurement component will be mitigated by other aspects of the overall remuneration package. The need for balance applies to all aspects of the performance measurement system, from the metric selection to target setting approach to the time horizon for evaluating performance (see Exhibit 9.1).

Consider a company operating in a highly cyclical industry, such as a temporary workforce provider. The results of the business are highly dependent on economic conditions—like unemployment rates—yet relative financial performance measurement is confounded by the fact that peer companies operate in very distinct geographies and industry spaces. For a company like this, a well-designed incentive program must

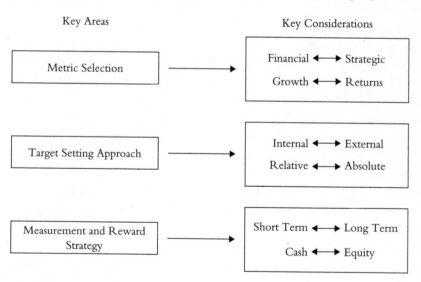

Figure 9.1 A Well-Balanced Performance Measurement System
SOURCE: Mercer.

incorporate multiple approaches to performance measurement, such as using both relative and absolute performance metrics and providing a balanced mix of both short-term and long-term incentives. By taking a holistic approach, potentially misleading results—such as the failure to meet absolute performance targets in an economic downturn—are either confirmed or contradicted by outcomes in other aspects of the performance measurement system—such as relative TSR performance against industry peers. This creates a system of "checks and balances" that reduces the likelihood that total remuneration outcomes will be out of kilter with performance and eliminates the need to tinker with incentive plans after the start of the performance cycle in the large majority of circumstances.

In addition to ensuring a well-balanced program design, there are specific design strategies that companies can use to add flexibility to the incentive program. As discussed in Chapter 5, the use of a scorecard enables companies to measure performance in a variety of areas deemed critical to the business. A scorecard approach has the added advantage of allowing specific metrics or weightings to be adjusted based on directional changes to the business strategy or customized to recognize distinct business unit priorities—without completely redesigning the incentive plan.

Similar frameworks can be developed to help companies deal with other types of organizational changes. One leading pharmaceutical multinational recently took such an approach. The company was interested in acquiring competitors regardless of their level of growth or their size. In preparation, they designed a new remuneration framework that could be applied differently based on the acquisition scenario. For example, small high-growth companies would be assigned a highly leveraged incentive model with an emphasis on variable pay that focuses key financial growth metrics. Meanwhile, more mature acquisitions would be placed into a less-leveraged incentive program that depended more heavily on the achievement of cost-containment and operational goals. The company could use the framework to quickly establish appropriate reward programs and help with the retention of key staff in the acquired companies.

Specific plan design features can also be incorporated to help manage external variability. For example, some companies have applied a banking concept to their short-term incentive plan to deal with industry cyclicality. In a banked incentive plan, a certain percentage of the award, or amounts above a specified level, are "banked" to provide a baseline award in future years. This approach smoothes the volatility of incentive awards by curtailing payouts in good years in order to bolster award levels during cycle downturns (see Exhibit 9.2).

Shareholder optics can be a challenge with this approach, as award levels may not be closely linked with immediate financial outcomes. Because of this, it is probably best reserved for cases where alternative

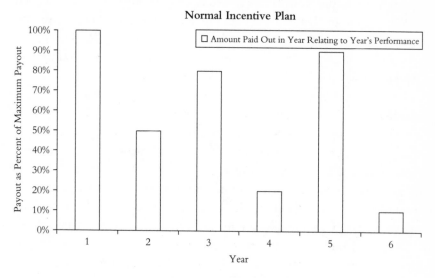

Normal Incentive Plan

□ Amount Paid Out in Year Relating to Year's Performance

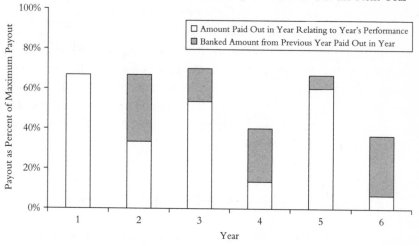

Banked Incentive Plan
One-Third of Award Is Banked Each Year and Paid Out the Next Year

□ Amount Paid Out in Year Relating to Year's Performance
■ Banked Amount from Previous Year Paid Out in Year

Exhibit 9.2   Normal Incentive Plan versus a Banked Incentive Plan
SOURCE: Mercer.

solutions, such as the use of relative performance measurement, are not a viable option. Still, banking can be a useful technique to counter sandbagging and avert an exodus of executive talent during lean years if shareholder communications are managed carefully.

Another strategy for addressing measurement challenges is to consider potential adjustments to metric definitions in an attempt to more accurately capture performance results. For example, consider a technology company that is implementing a major shift in business strategy. Significant investments in research and development (R&D) may be required up-front and the company may not fully realize a return for several years. While R&D expenditures are accounted for in the year that they occur under standard accounting rules, it may make more sense to amortize major investments over a longer period of time for purposes of assessing performance under executive incentive plans. By doing so, the company can encourage the investments needed to execute the business strategy and better match up outlays of capital with the expected period of expected return to more accurately measure performance.

Of course, any adjustments to metrics need to be spelled out clearly in advance and should not unfairly distort actual performance results. Companies must be prepared to explain to shareholders how specific incentive amounts were arrived at, and for this reason, it makes sense to limit the number of adjustments made. In addition, unusual metric definitions should be avoided when measuring performance on a relative basis since there would likely not be enough information to ensure an apples-to-apples comparison with peers.

By designing a well-balanced incentive program, and looking for ways to address performance measurement challenges up-front, companies can lessen the need to take corrective actions after the fact. This not only preserves the integrity of the remuneration program, but also reduced the administrative burden placed on the board, management, and human resource professionals.

Dealing with Unavoidable Adjustments

Even the most flexible incentive plan design will not preclude the need to make adjustments to the incentive plan on occasion. These adjustments can generally be grouped into three categories: (1) performance benchmark adjustments, which can be defined in the incentive plan; (2) performance benchmark adjustments that require case by case consideration; and (3) discretion applied to award outcomes after the fact.

No matter what type of adjustment is being considered, the same general principles should be used to guide decision making. First of all, what is the extent of the impact on performance and reward outcomes? If the impact is relatively minor or will be offset by other aspects of the incentive program, it is probably not worth making any adjustments to the performance benchmarks or award levels.

For example, if a company unexpectedly sells off an unprofitable portion of the business, there may be a negative impact on performance as measured by a growth metric, but a positive impact on performance as measured by profitability metrics. If the net impact on executive awards is negligible, no adjustments are warranted. But, even if there is a meaningful impact on short-term incentive payouts, adjustments may still not be necessary since the reduction in short-term incentive awards would presumably be offset by the increased value of equity awards (assuming the sale was effective in preserving or generating shareholder value).

If it is determined that the impact is meaningful and will not be offset by other aspects of the incentive program, the second criterion for making adjustments is that the impact is caused by a one-time occurrence, rather than a recurring event. For example, the financial results of a company that operates in both North America and Europe will be impacted by major shifts in currency exchange rates from time to time. One year, exchange rates may hurt results, while a few years later, results may be significantly helped. In this case, adjustments to performance targets or the use of discretion after the fact would be inappropriate, since there is a similar likelihood that executive awards would be impacted both positively and negatively.

If the impact is deemed to be both significant and extraordinary in nature, there must also be a consistent, objective, and defensible basis for making the adjustment. This is where incentive plan rules come into play. The treatment of incentive targets in certain common events, such as corporate transactions, should be spelled out in the rules of the incentive plan—even if such events are not likely in the near future. For example, a company might decide that, in the case of an acquisition, performance share goals will be adjusted proportionally if there is more than one year remaining in the performance period and the acquisition represents an increase of 30 percent or more in business value. In this way, both the criteria for the adjustment, as well as manner of the adjustment, are defined in advance.

If the cause of the adjustment cannot be anticipated, the company will need to develop a more comprehensive rationale behind performance target changes or discretionary adjustments to avoid criticisms of selectively manipulating incentive plan outcomes. It is not sufficient to say that the plan did not measure performance the way it was supposed to. You must be able to explain why measurement results are inaccurate and provide justification for why the adjustment selected is both necessary and reasonable. Shareholders are more than skeptical of inflated incentives in years when the value of their own investment declined, so the rationale must be compelling.

Let's take the example of the subprime mortgage crisis in the United States. Home-building suppliers are inordinately affected by the slowdown in new home construction, and if annual incentive plan targets were established based primarily on prior year results, there could be a very low likelihood that target or even threshold performance levels may be achieved in the current year. As a result, the motivational value of the annual incentive plan is limited and, in fact, the executive talent that you need to lead the company in this challenging time may be propelled to cut their losses and look for greener pastures elsewhere.

In this situation, the impact on performance results is meaningful and the cause is, presumably, a one-time event. But is an adjustment warranted? If shareholders are losing value, should not executives experience a significant reduction in remuneration as well? And if an adjustment is made, what should it look like? Unfortunately, there are no clear-cut answers. What makes sense for one organization may not be suitable for another.

If your remuneration program is well balanced overall, you may be able to rely on the motivational and retention value in your other incentive arrangements (such as equity awards) and let the short-term incentive plan payout based on the preestablished goals. This is the preferred approach for most companies, since it maintains a clear and objective relationship between business results and incentive pay based on the existing incentive plan design. In subsequent years, the company could consider ways to improve the accuracy of its performance measurement approach in the future, such as adding a relative performance component or focusing more on external developments during the target setting process.

If there is a real threat of losing executives, however, or if the company needs to refocus executive behaviors in direct response to the crisis, an adjustment to outstanding incentive awards may be apt. The most common adjustment would be to recast performance targets in light of newly available information. This requires careful deliberation and testing, as award outcomes must still appear reasonable in the eyes of shareholders.

Alternatively, additional information could be considered that provide for a more well-rounded assessment of performance. For example, relative performance could be considered to judge how the company performs relative to other similarly positioned businesses. Or a new metric could be introduced that aligns with the company's strategy for weathering the downturn.

In principle, new metrics or performance measurement approaches could be incorporated into the outstanding annual incentive award. However, it may be easier from a communication and administration standpoint to introduce a one-time supplemental award. Easier still, the additional information could simply be applied after the fact as the basis for making a discretionary adjustment to bonus payouts. The approach selected will depend on a company's specific objectives (for example, motivation versus retention), as well as technical considerations, such as the impact modifications or discretionary adjustments would have on the deductibility of incentive payments under the tax code.

The Question of Discretion

So far our discussion has focused on incentive plan adjustments that deal with unexpected or unusual events. But what about applying discretion to incentive plan results on a regular basis? Some companies use discretion as a way to recognize not only *what* results have been achieved, but also *how* those results were achieved. Performance that is viewed as sustainable and aligned with the company's strategic priorities is rewarded more favorably than results that emanate from temporary windfalls or reliance on obsolete business activities.

When relying on discretion as part of the regular performance measurement process, it is still best to specify the basis for such adjustments in advance to the extent possible. To accomplish this, some companies base the funding of short-term incentive awards on key financial goals, but use strategic "indicators" as the basis for making discretionary adjustments. For example, a company might use revenue growth as the financial metric, but identify strategic goals—such as a target amount of growth from key products or business lines—that will be used as the basis for fine-tuning award levels after the fact (see Exhibit 9.3). If executives achieve the revenue goal, but do so in a way that is not aligned with the go-forward business strategy, award levels can be reduced to reflect this.

This approach can be beneficial, but very difficult to execute in reality. Even with predefined indicators, the application of discretion still comes down to making a subjective judgment. Only those companies with highly effective governance and decision-making processes

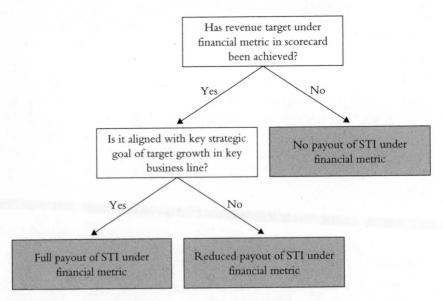

Exhibit 9.3 Flow Chart Illustrating Fine-Tuning of Award Levels
SOURCE: Mercer.

have the wherewithal to make discretionary adjustments that are consistent, fair, and defensible to executives and shareholders alike. In addition, the U.S. Internal Revenue Service does not treat incentive awards subject to upward discretionary adjustments as performance-based remuneration for the purposes of deductibility under Section 162(m) of the Internal Revenue Code. For these reasons, most companies reserve the use of discretion for making downward adjustments to awards only.

Dealing with Business Change

While adjustments to outstanding incentive plans are sometimes necessary to deal with unexpected developments, broader or more enduring changes often require companies to reevaluate their approach to performance measurement from a strategic perspective. To assist companies in undergoing such a review, we have identified several transformative events that may affect businesses and evaluated how real companies dealt with the challenges presented—both successfully and unsuccessfully. Each situation is different and must be addressed based on a company's unique business and organizational context, but as these case examples reveal, the executive remuneration program must be adapted from time to time to ensure that it continues to retain and reward management in a way that generates value for shareholders.

Hostile Takeover Offer

When a company receives an offer of a takeover, doubts can arise over what jobs will continue in the new company, at both a senior and junior level. This presents talent issues for both the target and the acquiring companies. The acquiring company will likely want to retain key talent to keep the company running prior to the takeover, while the target company will want to hold on to key talent should the takeover ultimately fail.

In one such situation, the Chief Financial Officer (CFO) of a company in the banking industry resigned in light of a potential takeover by any number of competitors. Loss of such a senior employee could negatively influence company performance, especially if the takeover is not ultimately successful. In this case, although a takeover was ultimately realized, the integration of the acquired company was made much more difficult by the loss of institutional knowledge and organizational leadership that resulted from the departure of the top financial executive.

Companies in this scenario should consider putting in place some form of a special retention incentive plan to encourage senior employees to stay throughout the transition. In designing such a plan, organizations should look for ways to link the retention awards to behaviors that will create the most value for shareholders. For example, companies might tie awards to the successful execution of critical integration initiatives.

Shareholders, as well as the media, are more likely to accept such a plan if payouts are conditioned on meeting specified performance criteria rather than simply linking payments to continued service. However, the payout of the plan and the targets have to be perceived as achievable and significant enough to encourage the executive to stay and reject other potentially lucrative offers from competitors. The type of retention plan is also something to consider, as a plan paid out in equity will be more in line with shareholder interests than one paid out in cash.

Resignation of Chief Executive

When a chief executive resigns, there is often a leadership race among the senior executives who all believe that they should take over this top job. Although the best candidate is usually chosen, other senior executives whose bids for the top post were not successful will likely feel dissatisfied. The future success of the company could be adversely affected if those executives who did not get the CEO role leave the company as a result. The company needs to be careful to ensure that these executives continue to be sufficiently engaged and motivated.

This can be particularly challenging when the departure of the CEO is unforeseen, as was the case with the unexpected resignation of the CEO at a large multinational company. Although one senior executive had long been branded as the likely successor to the CEO, the board awarded the role to a different member of the executive team. This prompted the immediate resignation of the first executive, leaving the company with a major talent gap in one of their most critical business areas and making the leadership transition that much more arduous.

In such situations, a company could consider offering a one-off incentive award to executives to help retain their service. This was the approach taken by one pharmaceutical company that recently awarded two of its top executives a substantial retention package to stay with the company despite losing out on the CEO role. The package consisted of a small cash payment and of shares handed out over a period of two to three years. While this strategy met with mixed results (one executive resigned just days after the package was announced and there has been shareholder criticism), it nevertheless represented an important strategic move to maintain the continuity of the business.

Whether there is a need to implement a special retention plan will depend on individual circumstances. Companies should consider the value of unvested long-term incentive awards that tie executives to the company, as an executive that is poised to receive a significant amount of equity in the near future will, though potentially disappointed about not getting the top job, be more likely to remain with the firm.

As with other types of retention incentives, shareholders are more likely to support the plan if awards are clearly linked to business results, either by means of share-based delivery or by attaching relevant performance conditions. In addition, a well-designed retention incentive may have the added advantage of communicating to a deflated executive their continued strategic importance to the business, and reiterating the economic opportunities that are available to them over the course of their career.

Divesting Part of the Business

Sometimes a company will decide to divest a significant part of the business, resulting in the senior management team running a smaller organization. Because remuneration opportunity is commonly linked to the size of the business, a question that arises is whether the executive remuneration package should be reduced in such a situation.

Consider the case of a major retail company that divested its newspaper and magazine distribution business. Despite the reduction in the size of the company's overall operations, the CEO retained the same salary and incentive packages. In fact, maximum bonus potential for the CEO was increased from 125 percent to 150 percent of salary. The company was reluctant to reduce the CEO's remuneration package, as significant value had been created via increases in share price and a return in cash to shareholders, thereby achieving the goals of the transaction as communicated to investors. Furthermore, a reduction in remuneration could have prompted the departure of the CEO from the company, and shareholders would be unlikely to want to lose the services of such a proven successful leader.

Organizational change can be a complex process and senior managers have to be given the proper incentives to carry it out successfully. A reduction in size of remuneration package is not necessarily aligned with the interests of shareholders if it serves as an obstruction to a value-creating event (like divesting a failing business) or if it results in unwanted executive turnover. Therefore, depending on the circumstances, a company should not necessarily reduce remuneration following a reduction in size of the business. Rather, as discussed in Chapter 6, the company should consider transitioning the peer group used for setting remuneration levels toward more appropriately sized companies gradually over time. In addition, various calibration techniques, such as the sharing ratio concept presented in Chapter 8, could be applied to confirm the reasonableness of current remuneration levels in light of performance outcomes.

Focusing Management on Emerging Markets

Apart from the retention implications, changing the nature of your business can also present challenges in shifting the strategic focus of executives. For example, increasing competition has led to a number of companies expanding their operations from their own country or region to include other parts of the globe. Should this change in business priorities be reflected in a new incentive arrangement?

One retail company in the United Kingdom grappled with this question when it unveiled plans that it would award its CEO an additional bonus of up to 2.5 million shares, with the payout tied exclusively to the success of the company's fledgling U.S. business. The new plan caused controversy among shareholders, with almost one in five shareholders rejecting the arrangement or abstaining from the vote. Why were shareholders and institutional advisory groups concerned?

Some shareholders were uncomfortable having a large payout linked to a single (and relatively minor) part of the business, especially considering that the annual bonus plan for the CEO was already amended to include it. Plus, incentive arrangements based on the company's overall business results (such as share-based awards) would seemingly capture and reward performance in overseas markets as well, potentially paying more than once for the same results. In the end, however, shareholders accepted the incentive plan in light of the company's strong historical performance results and growing concern over the retention of the CEO.

What could the retailer have done to prevent controversy? Shareholders generally understand that new incentive arrangements have to be put in place if current incentive plans appear to be uncompetitive. By explaining how the new incentive plan would impact the overall competitiveness of the CEO remuneration package, they may have allayed fears that the program would overpay based on results.

It also would have been constructive to explain how the incentive plan linked to the overall executive remuneration strategy, rather than treating it as a one-off award that affected the CEO in isolation. For example, they could have discussed how the new plan represented an evolution in remuneration policy that was meant to shift focus away from short-term financial results and toward the achievement of the company's strategic priorities, which includes creation of significant new business. Given this context, the company's statement that the plan had the flexibility to be expanded to include other potential business ventures may have been viewed in a positive light, rather than instigating fears that that a "yes" vote could result in an uncontrollable proliferation of incentive programs.

Turnaround Situation

When a company faces significant financial turmoil, it can be difficult to attract and retain the executive talent needed to alter the course of the business. In such cases, a special incentive plan may be offered to executives to motivate them to turn around an ailing company's fortunes. Such a plan requires measures that clearly demonstrate to the market and shareholders that performance has improved. Often, the focus of the turnaround strategy will be on improving operational results, with incentive plans typically linked to metrics such as margin improvement and cost savings.

One media company found itself in a turnaround situation after financial results fell drastically short of expectations and the company was forced into discussions with banks to avoid breaching some of its covenants. Within a day of the announcement, shares dropped by almost 20 percent to a 15-year low. The company's response was to implement a turnaround plan under a new leadership team. To motivate leadership to successfully execute the turnaround, a one-off incentive plan was introduced that would potentially produce a huge payout for executives if absolute share price targets were met.

Some shareholders felt that the absolute share price targets were not appropriate at the time when the plan was put in place; in fact, the first threshold share price target had already been met by the time it was communicated. Despite some opposition, the plan was established.

Shareholders will only agree to such a plan if performance targets will generate meaningful increases in shareholder value. Although the media company argued that absolute share prices were appropriate performance benchmarks due to transparency and clear line of sight, a relative market measure would likely have caused less controversy. Still better, operational metrics linked directly to the turnaround strategy may have been more successful at motivating the desired behaviors that would ultimately lead to a rebound in stock price.

Joint Ventures

A joint venture represents an interesting challenge to executive remuneration; how can you best motivate a group of executives who have come from different corporate cultures, each with different reward strategies? Some degree of integration is necessary to ensure that executives will be encouraged to work together to achieve common goals.

One example of successful integration of reward strategies occurred as part of a joint venture between a U.S. company and a Norwegian company in the industrial metals and mining industry. The U.S. company had in place a reward program that emphasized variable pay (via highly leveraged incentives), while the reward strategy of the Norwegian company was more focused on fixed pay. There was also a discrepancy in the level of remuneration received by executives at the two companies, with the total remuneration package for executives in the United States significantly higher than that of the Norwegian executives.

Since the joint venture was mainly going to be run by the Norwegian company, it was decided that an incentive program more aligned with European remuneration practices should be implemented. Globally consistent target and maximum bonus potentials were used, but base pay was determined based on benchmarking against the local market. One key objective of the reward program was to provide sufficient flexibility to adjust awards on an individual basis if actual incentive amounts resulted in some pay levels being uncompetitive or lower than the executive's remuneration opportunity prior to the venture.

This case example clearly shows the importance of flexibility when two very different reward cultures are brought together. A joint venture also has the complexity of taking into account the view of two different sets of shareholders and, in the case of cross-border ventures, the different regulatory environments the companies operate within. Often, it can be pragmatic to take a more conservative approach, while at the same time providing enough flexibility to adapt the program as specific situations require.

Supporting a Change in Business Strategy

Remuneration programs should be forward looking and reflect the strategic priorities of the company. Typically, a company's business strategy evolves over time and a review of incentive arrangements every two to three years is sufficient to keep the remuneration program relevant. This is not to say that major strategic shifts do not occur, and when they do, companies must be prepared to make significant changes to the incentive strategy to motivate executives to achieve the new strategic goals.

One example is of a leading retailer that developed a new business plan upon the arrival of a new CEO. The new plan was established to ensure that the company continues to produce strong financial results in face of an increasingly challenging market. A review of current remuneration was undertaken and concluded that a new incentive plan was required as those currently in place would have not sufficiently rewarded the stretching performance required to meet the new strategic goals. Therefore, to incentivize senior management to achieve their challenging goals, a one-off performance share plan was introduced in order to provide exceptional rewards if the superior levels of performance were achieved. Although there was some concern from shareholders about the quantum of the award, the plan was approved due to the high degree of linkage to highly stretching total shareholder return and profit growth goals.

Walking a Fine Line

Executive remuneration programs are constantly evolving to take into account external developments, as well as changes to the business strategy. Changes to incentive programs are typically small. However, there are exceptional circumstances that require a company to take more drastic steps.

Sometimes it can be hard to distinguish between events that are part of the norm for executives, and can therefore be addressed through existing incentive arrangements, and something that requires corrective action. Companies need to be able to treat their executives fairly, but must also remember that any changes must be reasonable in the eyes of shareholders. As the examples above show, shareholders will accept changes to the incentive program if those changes are aligned with the best interests of the company and ultimately lead to the creation of shareholder value.

Despite the best laid plans, the effectiveness of any executive reward program will depend on the ability of a company to respond to the measurement challenges that will inevitability arise. This underlies the importance of having clearly articulated objectives for your reward programs, as well as an effective decision-making process in place for dealing with complex and potentially sensitive problems in a manner that takes into account the interest of all relevant stakeholders.

Chapter 10

More Than the Sum of Its Parts

Bringing It All Together

Measuring the value your company creates can be as complex as determining how to create it. It is not enough for management to want to create value. They must define in specific terms what success *looks like*. What metrics will be used to gauge results? How much weight will be given to each strategic priority in evaluating performance, and how will the definition of success vary across different parts of the business? How will specific performance benchmarks be set, and what external reference groups—if any—will be used to gauge the difficulty of goals? How will the company distinguish between good and outstanding performance, and how will results be calibrated with incentive pay? And what happens when internal or external conditions change? How will the company respond to developments to ensure that the assessment process fairly reflects the circumstances under which the performance occurs?

These questions pinpoint the fundamental requirements of an effective performance measurement system (see Exhibit 10.1). As discussed throughout this book, each component of the measurement system—from metric selection to goal setting to award calibration—plays a critical role in translating the company's business strategy into action. By failing to approach measurement holistically, you run the risk of measuring the wrong things, or assessing results inaccurately or unfairly. Worse yet, your corporate processes will not reflect the priorities of the business and employee behaviors will not be aligned with the ultimate goal of shareholder value creation.

The design requirements outlined above are highly interdependent and work in concert to form a dynamic system. For example, the right metrics are only as good as the goals that are set. If you choose a return metric to encourage executives to focus on maximizing investments, but then set targets too high, executives may be incentivized to pass up economically profitable projects that could generate additional shareholder value. It is critical to understand how the value creation measures chosen interact with each other; there are often trade-offs that need to be understood up-front. Likewise, the effectiveness of an externally informed goal setting process depends on having a relevant and robust peer group. If

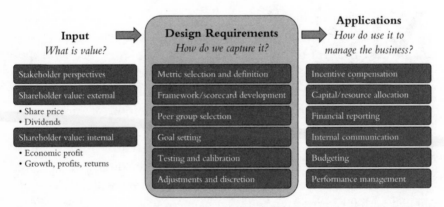

Exhibit 10.1 Performance Measurement System Design
SOURCE: Mercer.

you measure revenue growth relative to peers, but all of the peers are significantly larger than you or are in a market influenced by different economic factors, performance may appear artificially strong.

It may seem like a daunting task to adequately address all of these requirements, but developing a solid performance measurement system embedded in your company's unique business strategy is crucial to long-term business success. If you simply fall back on what the company has done in the past, or rely on what competitors are doing to manage and reward performance, your company will never maximize the full potential of the business.

In this chapter, we will discuss how you can put the principles and ideas discussed in Chapters 2 through 9 into play in your organization. While each component of the performance measurement equation is important, you do not have to take it all on at once. We will show you how to get started and begin the process of changing your business from one that passively manages and records results to one that actively manages the business with an eye to value creation.

Since the best laid plans fail without the right execution, we will also introduce some basic guidelines for implementing your performance measurement system once you have come up with the optimal design. Communication and education are paramount, but other factors, such as management buy-in and integration with a wide range of corporate processes, can often make or break the ability of the measurement system to drive real behavioral changes.

Finally, we have prepared a checklist to help guide you through the entire process, from value definition to system design to execution. By using this checklist to manage your efforts, you can ensure that the many benefits of an effective performance measurement system—for senior management, human resources and the board—will be realized by your organization.

Getting Started

Whether you have given significant thought to performance measurement in the past or are tackling it for the first time, it can be difficult to know where to start. Every company has embedded processes and procedures for monitoring, evaluating, and rewarding results, so even if you have never considered performance measurement formally, it is helpful to begin by evaluating how well your current remuneration programs capture and reward performance.

Before conducting any diagnostic analyses, you should identify the key stakeholders in assessing and refining the performance measurement system. Typically, human resources and finance will manage the collection and synthesis of quantitative and qualitative data under the direction of the compensation committee, CEO, or CFO. Alternatively, outside consultants may be retained to partner with human resources, or to work directly with the board or senior leadership in evaluating how well the current rewards program aligns with business results and to develop preliminary recommendations for improving the link between pay and performance. This approach enables the company to draw upon the specialized knowledge of remuneration experts and can also add greater objectivity to a highly sensitive undertaking. Such impartiality has benefits, foremost being that the outcomes of the process are likely to be more credible to both shareholders and employees.

Select members of the board and senior leadership team are usually called upon to provide qualitative input, particularly related to business strategy, shareholder considerations, and the external competitive landscape. The top executives, including the CEO, CFO, the head of human resources, and business unit leaders, can also provide valuable insight into matters such as organizational design, work culture, and talent needs. In addition, the CFO can help identify measurement challenges, such as limitations of the financial reporting system, and point out specific factors (e.g., off-balance sheet leases, nonrecurring special charges, etc.) that may necessitate careful interpretation of (or adjustments to) GAAP-based financial calculations.

Of course, senior leaders will have strong opinions about how well the current incentive programs reward executive performance from a *participant* perspective as well. Gathering participant feedback up-front, whether restricted to a small group or gathered more broadly through interviews, surveys or focus groups, can help ensure that the measurement system is not only theoretically sound, but that it will also be effective at motivating behaviors and driving change in the organization.

Once you have identified the major stakeholders who should be involved, we recommend initiating a two-pronged discovery process that will enable you to collect a range of pertinent information about existing performance measurement practices and identify key considerations arising from the business strategy. Start with a quantitative analysis of the company's historical relationship between pay and performance. The goal is to uncover potential misalignments, such as over- or underpayment of incentives or gaps in certain dimensions of performance relative to peers. The second step is to supplement this basic analysis with the collection of more qualitative input from members of the board and executive team. Through reflection and discussion, the story behind the data will begin to take shape.

Pay and Performance Diagnostic

A good pay and performance diagnostic includes metrics that align with all four categories in Mercer's performance measurement framework: growth, profits, returns, and shareholder experience (see Exhibit 10.2). Looking at performance over multiple time periods (typically, one and three years) gives you a sense of how the company is currently performing, as well as an understanding of directional performance trends.

A pay and performance diagnostic such as this can shed light on a variety of performance concerns. For example, by comparing financial results to external market performance, you can assess how well your business strategy is playing in the market place. If financial results are strong, but performance on shareholder-related metrics seems weak (as in the example in the previous section), the company may need to consider whether the strategy has been appropriately communicated to investors or if investors are rejecting the strategy outright as the wrong direction for the business. If the reverse is true (shareholder results appear stronger than financial performance), the company may want to pay close attention to shareholder assumptions about growth to ensure the current business plan does not fall short of these expectations.

In addition, relative performance analysis often uncovers gaps in performance that may warrant reevaluation of the company's strategic or operational priorities. For example, if a company finds that its position relative to peers on margin-related metrics has fallen unexpectedly over

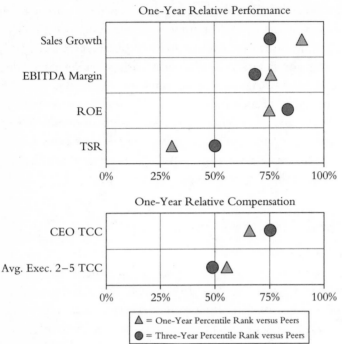

Exhibit 10.2   Sample Pay and Performance Diagnostic
SOURCE: Mercer.

the past three years, it may decide to implement a renewed emphasis on cost controls. Or, if the analysis reveals strong returns but weak revenue growth, the company may want to recast its measurement system to incentivize executives to look for new ways to invest in the growth of the business.

Looking at remuneration relative to peers in combination with performance results provides further insight about the effectiveness of the measurement system. Such comparisons provide an objective look at how competitively your current incentive plans reward executives given the company's performance and helps illuminate potential weaknesses in the target setting or calibration processes. The initial diagnostic may also hint at imbalances in the measurement framework, such as too much emphasis on short-term results, or insufficient focus on either the growth or return side of the value creation equation.

Analysis of this nature is usually best conducted by outside consultants, since they have access to both competitive financial performance data and historical remuneration information from peers. If managed internally, it can be conducted via the combined effort of corporate finance and human resources.

While a basic pay and performance diagnostic analysis cannot provide all the answers you need to refine your existing performance measurement system, it will enable you to formulate further questions for exploration. These questions will then help you determine the additional research and analyses necessary to draw robust and actionable conclusions.

Stakeholder Interviews

Interviews with key stakeholders in the business, including members of the board, executive team, and human resources, provide color commentary that allows you to more accurately interpret the diagnostic results. It can also help uncover issues that may not be apparent from historical analysis, such as limitations in the business strategy or latent concerns regarding talent retention, resource allocation, or other obstacles to value creation.

In determining who should be interviewed, strive to obtain a range of different perspectives while keeping in mind that the number of interviews should be kept to a manageable amount. If you interview too few stakeholders, you may miss critical input or fail to capitalize on the opportunity to gain buy-in from influential figures in the organization early in the process. Yet, if you interview too many people, summarizing and interpreting the many opinions gathered can become unwieldy and the costs can begin to outweigh the benefits.

As a general guideline, board interviews should include the board chair or lead independent director, compensation committee chair, and one or two other directors, while executive interviews should cover the CEO, CFO, CHRO (chief human resources officer), business unit heads, and one or two other executives who can provide high-level insight into the company's business priorities. At a manufacturing firm, this might mean the COO (chief operations officer) or top manufacturing executive, while at a technology company, the CTO (chief technology officer) or top engineering executive may be in a position to provide more useful input.

A comprehensive interview typically covers three key areas: business strategy, performance measurement issues, and organizational design and talent requirements. While some questions are universally relevant, to the extent possible the interview should be tailored to your company's unique internal and external context, as well as the specific role of the interviewee. Exhibit 10.3 provides some sample interview questions that might be used as part of the initial discovery process.

Again, an outside consultant may be hired to help administer the interviews and compile the preliminary findings. Otherwise, this role is often assigned to a member of the human resource team, as many HR professionals have strong expertise in the areas of communication and facilitation that they can draw upon in collecting and synthesizing a range of diverse perspectives.

The information gathered through this type of qualitative research coupled with the quantitative analysis of historical pay and performance outcomes discussed earlier enables a company to develop a plan of action for refining the performance measurement system, or in some cases, redesigning it from a blank slate. The process also helps companies to prioritize their actions, building in a realistic time frame and allocating the resources necessary to undertake plan design and implementation.

Semico Case Study

To get a better idea of how these preliminary steps might help set the stage for further discovery, and eventual plan redesign and implementation, consider the case study of a midsize semiconductor company. Semico, like other companies in the industry, experienced a period of extensive performance decline during the late 1990s that resulted from an oversaturation of the market and dwindling demand from key customers in the telecommunications industry. The company's strategy for weathering the storm was to drastically cut spending and sell off underutilized property and equipment in an effort to bolster investor

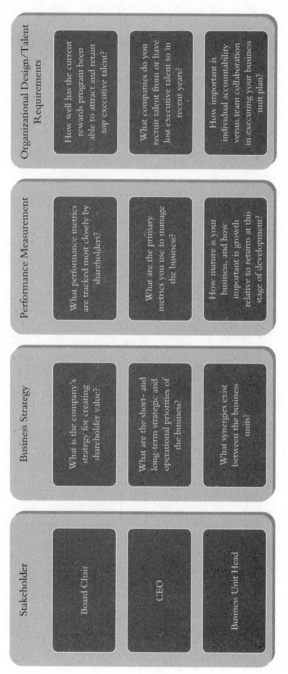

Exhibit 10.3 Sample Interview Questions by Stakeholder

SOURCE: Mercer.

confidence and generate sufficient cash to tide the business over until
market demand rebounded.

In time, Semico saved up millions of dollars in cash, and by 2003,
its liquid reserves equaled more than half of its total market value.
A diagnostic analysis of its short- and long-term performance against
peers (see Exhibit 10.4) suggested that while the company had performed reasonably well on profitability and return measures, its growth
was dismal. Contrary to what management expected, shareholders did

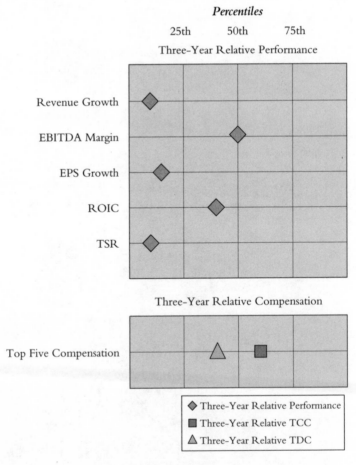

Exhibit 10.4   Semico Pay and Performance Diagnostic
SOURCE: Mercer.

not seem to value the company's fiscally conservative strategy, and instead punished the company by rapidly selling off shares.

When remuneration was taken into consideration, further problems were revealed. Since the company's incentive plan was based on a profit-sharing model, executives continued to receive competitive annual incentive payments, despite declines in shareholder performance. And, while actual gains under the stock option plan were minimal due to the drop in stock price, the company had been forced to grant more and more options in the name of retention, prompting negative ratings by shareholder advisory groups.

Interviews with directors and senior executives highlighted additional challenges faced by Semico. While directors expected management to use the company's cash to fund a major acquisition or merger with a similarly sized competitor that could provide access to broader markets and complementary products and technologies, the management team had been focusing on smaller, accretive acquisitions to gradually build up the capabilities of the organization in its core products over time. In addition, the Chief Technology Officer revealed a dangerous gap in Semico's strategy: while the company's contracts depended highly on its brand reputation as a provider of high-quality, customizable circuitry solutions, cuts in the areas of research and development and field staff were seriously threatening Semico's competitive advantage in these areas.

The results of the pay and performance diagnostic, coupled with input from key stakeholders, enabled the company to identify several important questions about the current performance measurement system (see Exhibit 10.5) and to prioritize its efforts for refining the system to better support the company's value creation efforts.

As a result of the discovery process, Semico decided to shift the emphasis of its short-term incentive plan from profitability to a balance of profit and growth metrics and to analyze the costs and benefits of eliminating stock option awards in favor of performance shares that might more effectively reward long-term financial performance. In addition, it determined that the company's strategic objectives— including those related to the use of the cash reserves to fuel inorganic growth—needed to be better defined and more explicitly incorporated into the performance measurement process.

Metric Selection and Definition

- Does the current measurement system discourage investments to fuel growth by placing too much emphasis on profitability?
- To what extent should strategic objectives, such as inorganic growth through acquisition, be incorporated into measurement processes?

Framework Development

- Is the profit-sharing plan too narrow in focus to accurately capture short-term results?
- Should the company consider supplementing or replacing option grants with performance-based equity conditioned on meeting the company's long-term financial goals?

Peer Group Selection

- How might the peer group need to be changed going forward as the company uses its cash to grow the business and enter new markets?

Goal Setting

- Does the current goal setting process sufficiently recognize external business context, such as competitor performance?

Testing and Calibration

- How should threshold, target, and superior performance levels be established during the turnaround?

Adjustments and Discretion

- In what ways might performance measurement be affected by a major acquisition? Are adjustments to metric definitions necessary?

Exhibit 10.5   Key Questions Resulting from Semico's Initial Diagnostics

SOURCE: Mercer.

Determining the Next Steps

The questions that come out of the initial diagnostic enable a company to define a plan of attack. While Semico determined that their measurement system needed a major overhaul, many companies discover that their programs are functioning reasonably well and simply need fine-tuning in a few select areas. Armed with an initial needs assessment, your company will be able to develop a tactical approach to refining the performance measurement system and keeping it current over time.

In developing a work plan to review and refine the performance measurement system at your own company, consider the following steps:

1. Prioritize your measurement needs based on the questions that arise from the initial diagnostic, as well as practical considerations, such as the corporate calendar and scheduled compensation committee meetings.
2. Define the data necessary to inform the design process and select the specific research and analyses that will generate this information.
3. Identify the primary stakeholders in the process and assign roles and responsibilities for synthesizing the data and drawing conclusions.
4. Establish a timeline for completing the work.

Finally, remember that designing a winning measurement system is only half of the battle. You must allot sufficient time and resources to execute a comprehensive implementation strategy, including education and ongoing communication with both executives and shareholders.

The Implementation Road Map

While this book focuses primarily on design, you should not underestimate the importance of implementation when tackling performance measurement at your organization. Many companies invest heavily in developing a new measurement system only to roll out the program with a simple e-mail or memo. A narrow approach like this will simply not work. In order to really drive a value creation mind-set, companies must progress from merely collecting and disseminating information, to providing insight, generating impact, and, finally, institutionalizing the measurement system into day-to-day decision making (see Exhibit 10.6).

Information

Performance measurement systems are based largely on information sharing. Because information is the foundation for measuring and rewarding performance, implementation of the measurement plan often begins by considering how information will be collected and disseminated. How will performance results be tracked, and at what levels? In what ways will information be communicated throughout the organization, and at what frequency? The answers to these types of questions set the strategy for empowering employees through information.

Insight

The next stage of implementation involves distilling information down into something with greater meaning and applicability for executives and employees as they go about their jobs. This action transforms

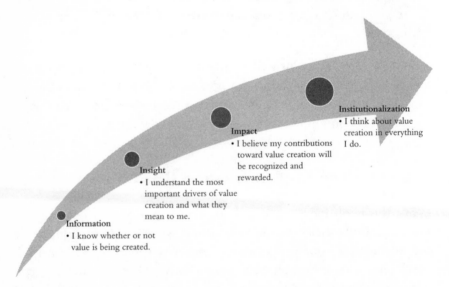

Exhibit 10.6   Stages in Implementing a Performance Measurement System
SOURCE: Mercer.

information into insight and brings the human capital strategy into alignment with the business strategy. As we have discussed throughout this book, an effective measurement system depends on identifying and prioritizing the drivers of value creation. These core value drivers serve as the basis for the performance measurement framework.

Impact

Insight turns into impact for the organization when the performance measurement framework is applied to hold people accountable for results. The ways an organization measures success should translate into how it rewards for results. This means taking insights about value creation and using them to direct incentive compensation and performance management programs. It is often said that "what gets measured gets done"— and this is especially true if you get rewarded for what gets measured.

Institutionalization

Institutionalization is the ultimate goal of the implementation process. It requires integrating the performance measurement system into all aspects of business management, not just incentive payments and performance reviews. When the performance measurement system has been institutionalized, executives and employees at all levels of the organization understand how their day-to-day activities impact results and base decision making on the singular objective of value creation. By extension, institutionalization also helps individuals to more clearly see the connection between their performance and pay.

Getting to the point where the measurement system has been institutionalized into the corporate culture and organizational processes takes significant investment, especially if the measurement system represents a major divergence from the status quo. Substantial up-front training to educate executives about the measurement process is usually necessary. Executives need to understand how the organization creates value, what metrics are used to measure that value creation, and how value creation is affected by specific activities within the business. The message must be clear, consistent, and tailored appropriately to the needs and competencies of the audience. The training of senior executives should not be the same as training lower down in the organization, just as training in one business unit or geography may look different than training in the next depending on the role played by each in the value creation process.

To build on the knowledge delivered through up-front education efforts, companies must adopt a strategy for reinforcing the teachings using consistent ongoing communication. A variety of modalities should be experimented with, recognizing that not all people learn in the same way. One executive might skim over an e-mail communication, while another might appreciate the ability to access such information on the road. The former may prefer a face-to-face meeting with senior management, while the latter may view the meeting as an imposition on his or her busy schedule.

To the extent possible, communication should be put in terms of what the measurement system means for each individual. Talking generically about strategic plans or incentive programs is never as compelling as spelling out how the strategy will be executed through an individual's own job or quantifying a person's actual compensation opportunity. The best communications always strive to answer the question, "What is in it for me?"

In addition to communication and education, there are other factors that influence a company's ability to transform the impact of the measurement system from information to institutionalization. Like other change management initiatives, the cooperation and support of senior leadership is critical. Companies should never wait until the measurement system is finalized to start garnering such support; management buy-in should be a top priority early on in the process. One of the best ways to ensure everyone will be on board with the new measurement system is to gather input broadly during the design phase. Individual interviews or focus groups go a long way in making members of the management team confident that their interests and opinions have been reflected in the final product.

Along with management support, deep and broad application of the measurement system will help facilitate a collective mind-set focused on value creation. As discussed in Chapter 3, the measurement system is embedded in numerous corporate processes. If your company fails to apply the new measurement system beyond incentive compensation, it will never be successful in driving change. The measurement system should also be actively incorporated into activities like budgeting, investment allocation, performance management, and external reporting. Only after executives see the measurement system at work in the larger organization will they allow it to guide their own activities.

Finally, the measurement system must be reviewed and updated frequently to ensure it does not lose relevance to the organization over time. If the measurement system emphasizes growth, but the CEO is encouraging executives to rein in spending, confusion will set in and the measurement system will be abandoned as a guiding force in the organization. Measurement is a cyclical process, and care must be taken to monitor measurement outcomes and adjust the parameters of performance measurement as needed to keep the system up to date.

One way to ensure that the measurement system is kept current is to conduct the pay and performance diagnostic introduced earlier in the chapter on an annual basis. This is often best done in conjunction with reviewing the company's business plan or executive remuneration programs. It provides a simple gauge of a company's performance against peers and can often uncover weaknesses in the current measurement system or potential misalignments between pay and performance outcomes before they get out of hand.

The pay and performance diagnostic can also be used as a tool to communicate results to executives and shareholders. It serves as a high-level dashboard that monitors how well the business strategy is being translated into financial and market success. Using the diagnostic for multiple purposes helps achieve a level of consistency necessary to affect the institutionalization of the measurement system.

The Benefits of a Performance Measurement Mind-Set

Designing and implementing a performance measurement system takes time and effort but if done properly, the returns will most certainly outweigh the costs. The advantages of a well-designed and fully institutionalized measurement system are numerous; senior management, the board of directors, and human resources all benefit in different ways from sound performance measurement processes.

For senior management, the measurement framework becomes a tool to communicate the strategic vision of the organization and run the business. Added clarity around those factors that are most closely linked to value creation generally leads to greater efforts by employees in the areas that matter most. By aligning the organization toward the singular goal of value creation, individuals at every level of the organization are empowered to make the difficult decisions that determine business success. The measurement system also helps facilitate a greater sense of commitment to the organization, since rewards are tied to factors that executives and employees feel they can influence.

The process of designing the performance measurement system almost always fosters a better understanding of the link between human capital programs and policies and business strategy execution. This benefits members of the human resource function by better positioning them to be strategic advisors to the executive team. It also gives human resources a more profound understanding of the business strategy, which enables them to develop more effective programs in areas such as recruiting, training, and organizational development.

Because the performance measurement system serves as the basis for the company's rewards programs, it enables human resources to design competitive remuneration packages that have the ability to attract and retain the right talent to the organization. It also serves as a foundation for pushing incentive programs down throughout the organization, helping to build a pay-for-performance mentality at all levels of the company.

There are numerous benefits for the compensation committee and board of directors as well. A well-designed measurement system ensures the fiduciary responsibility of the board is being met by shepherding the relationship between pay and performance in a way that maximizes shareholder value creation. It also provides an objective and defensible basis for decision making, which makes it easier to articulate the rationale behind specific remuneration outcomes. This facilitates the clear and transparent disclosure of executive remuneration programs, a cornerstone of good governance.

In today's environment of heightened sensitivity and economic uncertainty, companies cannot afford to *not* invest the time and effort required to get the performance measurement system right. Good governance is on everyone's lips, and those companies that do not exhibit strong governance practices are being rebuked by shareholders and regulators through various initiatives intended to strike a blow at board autonomy. "Say-on-pay" is already a reality in Australia, the United Kingdom, and some parts of continental Europe, and may be on the horizon in the United States and elsewhere. Companies that take the time to get their systems in line now will be much better positioned to secure a "yes" vote from shareholders when the need arises.

More importantly, however, the right performance measurement system will help propel value creation. Research shows that the most successful companies tie a greater percentage of their remuneration to performance (Exhibit 10.7), and those companies that focus executives on the key factors that drive value creation are best positioned to achieve financial and market success.

Having executives work at cross purposes quickly erodes any competitive advantage you have in the marketplace and makes it difficult to capitalize on new opportunities as they arise. Instead, use the measurement system to get everyone aligned behind the singular objective of

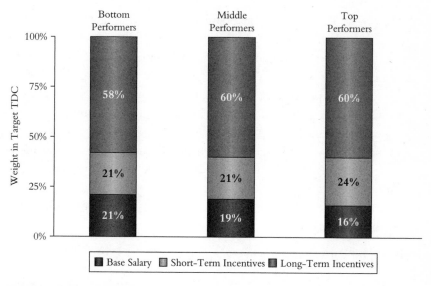

Exhibit 10.7 CEO Pay Mix by Performance Groups
SOURCE: Mercer.

value creation. With a value creation mind-set, the right decisions will fall into place. Executive remuneration is a big investment, and you should maximize the return on your investment by using it as a tool to communicate and reinforce the strategic priorities of the business.

Convinced? Great! The checklist that follows this chapter will help you put the principles introduced throughout this book into practice. Take the first step today to transform your company into a nimble, purposeful organization that aligns its people and process behind the ultimate goal of value creation.

Bringing It All Together: A Performance Measurement Checklist

Getting Started (Chapter 1)

- ❏ Conduct a diagnostic analysis of financial and market performance (i.e., growth, profits, returns, and TSR) and executive pay (i.e., total cash compensation and total direct compensation) relative to peers over one- and three-year periods.
- ❏ Identify any misalignment between pay and performance outcomes based on the diagnostic analysis.
- ❏ Interview members of the board of directors to gather their perspective on the strengths and weaknesses of the current performance measurement system and related incentive programs.
- ❏ Interview members of the senior executive team to gather insight on historical performance results, the go-forward business strategy, short- and long-term strategic priorities, and the current performance measurement system and incentive programs.
- ❏ Pinpoint key questions arising from the diagnostic analysis and interviews and identify additional research needed to inform the design process.
- ❏ Prioritize needs, develop a work plan, assign responsibility, and establish a time line for completion.

Value Definition (Chapters 2 and 3)

- ❏ Identify organizational stakeholders and explore competing definitions of value creation.

❏ Agree on a definition of shareholder value creation for the organization (*Note:* this may include both an internal and external definition).

Metric Selection (Chapter 4)

❏ Define the universe of relevant performance metrics based on Mercer's measurement framework (growth, profits, returns, and shareholder experience).
❏ Use qualitative analysis to uncover the key drivers of performance:
  - Identify the company's profit model and articulate the strategic plan for maximizing competitive advantage.
  - Conduct a value chain analysis to identify the various factors that influence value creation throughout the organization.
❏ Use quantitative analysis to assess how well potential financial metrics capture value creation:
  - Use regression analysis to analyze the correlation between various financial metrics and shareholder value creation.
  - Conduct a performance sensitivity analysis to understand how corporate, industry, and market-wide forces impact external value.
  - Perform a time series analysis of key financial measures to pinpoint performance improvement opportunities and investigate performance trends.
  - Analyze economic profitability across various business units to inform the degree of customization required below the corporate level.
❏ Evaluate potential metrics based on the quantitative and qualitative analyses discussed above, as well as the following considerations:
  - Does the metric reflect a reasonable trade-off between accuracy and complexity?
  - Is the metric suitable for measuring short- or long-term performance (or both)?
  - Does the metric (alone or in combination with other metrics) appropriately recognize the trade-offs between growth and returns?
  - Is the metric applicable across the business, or is it relevant only for certain business units?

- ■ Does the metric allow for meaningful comparisons against peers?
- ■ Can the metric be tracked using our current financial reporting systems?
- ❏ Select a combination of metrics that will be used to measure performance over both the short and long term (*Note:* metrics may be financial, operational, or strategic in nature).
- ❏ Consider potential adjustments that might enhance the ability of the metric to fairly and accurately capture performance results and test the suitability of alternative metric definitions.

Framework Design (Chapter 5)

- ❏ Analyze the line of sight between various executive roles and the metrics selected for the performance measurement system.
- ❏ Determine the appropriate linkage (e.g., corporate, business unit, group, etc.) at which performance should be measured for various executive roles based on line of sight and other organizational considerations.
- ❏ Identify the key success factors that contribute disproportionally to success and use this information to prioritize and assign weights to the selected metrics (*Note:* prioritization may differ across business units).
- ❏ Develop a flexible framework, such as an unbalanced scorecard, for applying metrics, weightings, and linkage to manage and reward executive performance at various levels in the organization.

Peer Group Development (Chapter 6)

- ❏ Establish criteria for selecting peers using the following categories:
  - ■ Markets (customer, labor, capital)
  - ■ Size
  - ■ Business characteristics
- ❏ Apply the criteria identified to screen potential peers for similarity to the company.
- ❏ If the selection process results in too few peers, consider the following actions to expand the potential universe of peers:

- Conduct a performance sensitivity analysis to identify capital market peers that have similar levels and degrees of company-specific, industry, and market risk.
- Look for businesses in other industries with similar business character.
- Identify companies that are upstream or downstream from your business.
- Consider competitors operating in other geographies.
☐ Consider the need for adopting a secondary peer group to supplement information gathered from primary peers.
☐ Clarify how peer group data will be collected and used for analyzing pay magnitude, informing remuneration plan design, measuring performance, and/or setting performance targets.
☐ Review and revise the peer group every three years, or earlier if undergoing a major strategic or organizational change.

Target Setting (Chapter 7)

☐ Select a strategy for setting performance targets based on business context and availability of data. (*Note:* a combination of approaches may be appropriate.)
☐ If using externally informed target setting, collect data from a variety of internal and external, historical, and prospective sources:
- Analyst expectations for the company and its peers.
- Historical performance data for the company and its peers.
- Macroeconomic indicators.
- Analysis of shareholder expectations.
- Management forecasts and budgets.
☐ Synthesize inputs to set achievable, yet meaningful performance targets that have approximately a 50 percent chance of being realized.
☐ If using relative performance measurement, determine how performance will be assessed against peers (e.g., step ranking versus percentile ranking versus some other comparative process).
☐ Determine how the relative measurement process will be adapted if the peer group changes during performance period (e.g., as a result of mergers or acquisitions).

Leverage, Calibration, and Testing (Chapter 8)

❑ Determine the appropriate relationship between risk and reward for your company by considering factors such as business strategy and talent requirements.

❑ Calibrate threshold and upside performance targets to achieve the desired leverage in your incentive plans:

  ■ Select the appropriate probability of achieving of threshold and superior performance levels based on your risk-reward profile and the competitiveness of the incentive opportunity delivered.

  ■ Collect internal and external input to inform the payout curve design.

  ■ Test the payout curve design using simulation modeling.

❑ Use simulation modeling to assess the value and opportunity associated with various long-term incentive vehicles.

❑ Select incentive delivery vehicles (cash, stock options, performance shares, etc.) based on desired leverage and alignment with the metrics selected to gauge performance.

❑ Set incentive caps at appropriate levels.

❑ Test the reasonableness of incentive plans by calculating the entire range of potential outcomes and analyzing historical and prospective TSR sharing ratios relative to peers.

Adjustments and Discretion (Chapter 9)

❑ Review the performance measurement framework for fairness by ensuring it captures multiple dimensions of performance.

❑ Consider opportunities to enhance the flexibility of the incentive plan designs (e.g., apply banking concept, incorporate measure adjustments, etc.).

❑ Brainstorm the types of developments that might warrant adjustments to the measurement system or processes and develop a set of guiding principles for addressing such issues.

❑ Consider how discretion should be used in your organization (if at all) and establish guidelines for its usage.

❑ Proactively address specific measurement challenges (corporate transactions, change in business strategy, etc.) as they arise.

Implementation (Chapter 10)

❑ Secure senior management buy-in early on by gathering and incorporating their feedback into the design process.

❑ Invest in educating executives about value creation and the measurement system prior to rolling out new incentive plans.

❑ Develop an ongoing communication strategy to support initial training efforts.

❑ Communicate using a variety of modalities with an eye to answering the question, "What is in it for me?"

❑ Look for ways to incorporate the measurement system into a wide variety of corporate processes so as to institutionalize a value creation mind-set.

❑ Review the performance measurement system frequently and make changes as needed to ensure it does not go stale over time.

❑ Provide clear and transparent disclosure of the performance measurement system to shareholders, including how the measurement system is used as a basis for remuneration decisions.

About the Authors

MERCER

Mercer is a leading global provider of consulting, outsourcing, and investment services. Mercer works with clients to solve their most complex benefit and human capital issues, designing and helping manage health, retirement, and other benefits. It is a leader in benefit outsourcing. Mercer's investment services include investment consulting and multi-manager investment management. Mercer's 18,000 employees are based in more than forty countries. For more information, visit www.mercer.com

Contributors

David Carlin is a senior associate in Mercer's London office. His experience includes working with a range of multinational companies on executive remuneration issues including the design of incentive programs and performance measure selection and calibration. Mr. Carlin received a Masters in Mathematical Engineering from Bristol University.

Diane L. Doubleday, a worldwide partner, is the global leader of the executive remuneration service segment and located in Mercer's London office. She works with clients and colleagues to consider the business, performance, regulatory and governance implications of executive total remuneration to drive business performance and value creation, secure key talent, and withstand external scrutiny. Ms. Doubleday earned her B.A. and J.D. from the University of California, Berkeley.

William H. Ferguson, a worldwide partner, is Mercer's human capital market business leader for the Pacific Southwest and a member of the human capital Americas Business Leadership Group. He advises senior management and boards of directors on how to create shareholder value by designing high-impact value management, performance measurement, and compensation programs. Mr. Ferguson received a B.A. in Economics and International Relations and an M.S. in Engineering-Economic Systems from Stanford University.

Thomas Flannery is a principal in Mercer's Boston office. He has significant experience working with clients in the for-profit and not-for-profit sectors, assisting them with executive and employee compensation as well as succession planning and performance management. Mr. Flannery received a Doctor of Philosophy in Public Policy and Administration from Northwestern University.

Yolande Foord is a principal and the executive remuneration service segment leader for Australia and New Zealand. Based in the Melbourne office, Yolande also has worked in Mercer's San Francisco, Sydney, London, and Dublin offices. Her global consulting experience includes executive compensation strategy and design, annual and long-term incentive plan design, and performance measurement consulting. Ms. Foord received a Bachelor of Commerce in Finance and Law, and a LL.B. from the University of Pretoria, South Africa.

Bruce D. Greenblatt is a principal in Mercer's Philadelphia office. He works with boards of directors and senior management on designing executive remuneration and performance measurement programs that align rewards with business objectives. Mr. Greenblatt received a B.S. in Economics from the Wharton School of the University of Pennsylvania and holds a J.D. from the University of Pennsylvania Law School.

Michael J. Halloran is a worldwide partner and located in Mercer's Dallas office. He works with boards of directors and senior management to ensure their executive remuneration programs support the organization's strategic and financial objectives in order to create shareholder value. Mr. Halloran has a bachelor's degree in Mathematics from Northwestern University and an M.B.A. in Finance and Accounting from Northwestern's Kellogg School.

Mark W. Hoble is a principal in Mercer's London office. He advises clients on executive compensation strategy and design and, as a member of Mercer's global M&A team, has a particular expertise around executive compensation in private equity transactions. Mr. Hoble earned an M.B.A. from London Business School and a B.A. in Economics from the University of Nottingham.

Martín M. Ibañez Frocham, located in Mercer's Buenos Aires office, is a worldwide partner and the executive remuneration service segment leader for Latin America. Martin's experience combines consulting and line management and includes the design of executive and broad-based incentive compensation plans. Mr. Ibañez Frocham received a B.S. and M.S. in Pharmacy and Biochemistry from the University of Buenos Aires and an M.B.A. from CEMA Buenos Aires.

Daniel S. Laddin is a principal in Mercer's New York office. He works with boards of directors and senior management in the areas of executive compensation, performance measurement, and incentive plan design. Mr. Laddin received his M.B.A. from the University of Chicago Graduate School of Business and B.S. in Accounting from the University of Albany.

Gregg H. Passin is a principal in Mercer's New York office and leader of the executive remuneration segment's work in ownership and private equity transactions. He counsels companies on global executive compensation and corporate governance issues relating to senior executives, boards of directors, and professional services firm partners and professionals. Mr. Passin received a B.A. in History from Yale and an M.B.A. from the Wharton School of the University of Pennsylvania.

Piia Pilv is a principal and located in Mercer's Geneva office. She specializes in global executive compensation, particularly executive remuneration strategy and stock-based long-term incentive plan design. Ms. Pilv holds an M.B.A. from the London Business School and a B.A. in Economics from the Barnard College, Columbia University.

Lisa M. Slipp, located in Mercer's Toronto office, is a worldwide partner and the executive remuneration service segment leader for Canada. She works with boards of directors and senior management to ensure their executive remuneration plans align pay with corporate performance and create shareholder value. Ms. Slipp has a B.A. from the University of Western Ontario and an M.B.A. from York University.

Jennifer Wagner is a principal in Mercer's San Francisco office. She specializes in global executive remuneration, equity strategy, and performance measurement consulting. Ms. Wagner graduated with a B.A. in Sociology from the State University of New York at Geneseo and is a Certified Compensation Professional and Senior Professional in Human Resources.

Index